Justice-Involved Youth

Including a peer-support workbook with exercises, this book demonstrates the therapeutic value of art practice, both inside and outside institutions, as a more humane approach for children and adolescents affected by mass incarceration. The author discusses how a trauma-informed approach can heal marginalized and ignored citizens and refutes the notion that severe punishment for repeat offenders is essential or effective.

Author Carol Cross has decades of experience incorporating therapeutic expressive arts in her professional practice, with a focus on peer-led programs. She advocates a trauma-informed approach using a peer-driven creative process, showing how such programs can intervene in the cycle of violence and contribute to a practice of community preventive care for youth deemed to be at risk. The workbook is built on the research and resources Cross has used within care plans with clinical teams and youth forensics. The user is shown how to build on these teachings and implement or modify the content to suit individual needs. Contributions from persons involved in the judicial system and such intervention programs vet the topics in the workbook as resonating with group participants.

This user-friendly book will benefit anyone working with justice-involved children and adolescents, including those working in and around the criminal legal system as well as in programs outside of carceral institutions organized by individuals, groups, or non-profit organizations.

Carol Cross, PhD, has professional experience that includes introducing arts experiences in nontraditional settings, working with adults and adolescents experiencing homelessness or incarceration, and with at-risk and high-risk youth. She has also taught at the university level. A visual artist and educator, Cross holds a Bachelor of Fine Arts from the Emily Carr University of Art + Design, Vancouver, British Columbia. Her Master's thesis focused on the social benefits of establishing sustainable community programs, and education as social intervention for youths at risk. In her efforts to build positive social change and early intervention in schools, and raise awareness of violence as a social problem, she set up a free, after-school photography and writing program for teens at risk in Vancouver with the support of Provincial and Government of Canada funding. Awarded a Government of Canada contract, she began working with incarcerated male and female teens in British Columbia. Her doctoral research, a qualitative study, examined critical pedagogy, adolescent development, and research into the governance and policies surrounding incarcerated male and female youth. She is the author of *Juvenile Justice and Expressive Arts: Creative Disruptions through Art Programs for and with Teens in a Correctional Institution*. She holds a PhD from the University of Victoria.

Justice-Involved Youth

Healing Through Trauma with Creativity and Community Regeneration + Peer-Support Workbook

Carol Cross

Routledge
Taylor & Francis Group
NEW YORK AND LONDON

Designed cover image: "Cycloptic Merman," 2016, by Chris "Daze" Ellis, Sam Wisneski, and students from Thrive Collective.
Cover Photograph: "Coney Island Mural", 2018, by Carol Cross

First published 2025
by Routledge
605 Third Avenue, New York, NY 10158

and by Routledge
4 Park Square, Milton Park, Abingdon, Oxon, OX14 4RN

Routledge is an imprint of the Taylor & Francis Group, an informa business

ISBN: 978-1-032-87716-7 (hbk)
ISBN: 978-1-032-87715-0 (pbk)
ISBN: 978-1-003-53408-2 (ebk)

DOI: 10.4324/9781003534082

Typeset in Sabon
by KnowledgeWorks Global Ltd.

Access the Support Material: https://resourcecentre.routledge.com/books/9781032877150

Contents

List of Figures *viii*
Preface *ix*
About the Thrive Collective *xi*

1 Setting the Stage 1

Introduction 1
Trauma and Healing through Creative Expression 2
Cognitive Conflict 2
Democracy and Creativity 3
Resiliency and Recovery 3
Trauma and Suicide 4
Pharmacological Treatment and Young Offenders 5
Why Art Matters 5
Personal Healing and Creativity 6
Conclusion 7

2 Social Justice: Shifting Powers 10

Introduction 10
Reform and Advocacy: Post Traumatic Stress Disorder (PTSD) 10
Wellbeing and the Expressive Arts 11
The Link between Childhood Experience and Delinquency 12
Intergenerational Trauma 13
The Youth Criminal Justice Act – Canada 13
Fetal Alcohol Syndrome Disorder (FASD) 14
BIPOC (Black, Indigenous, People of Color) and Culturally-Sensitive Support 15
The Nelson Mandela Rules 16
Youth Culture and Incarceration 16
Growing Up Behind Bars 17
PTSD and Rehabilitation 19

Youth Development Theory and Incarceration 21
Substance Use Disorder and Street Life 21
Intersection between Mental Health and the Juvenile Justice System 23
The Resource Guide 24
Conclusion 25

3 Community Regeneration: Making the Connection 27

Introduction 27
Community Justice 27
Incarceration versus Community 28
Emotional Development 28
Art as Education and Therapy 29
The 'Business' of Incarceration 29
Social Intelligence and Collaboration 30
Culturally Responsive Programs 30
Social Inclusion and Mental Health 31
Conclusion 31

4 Community as a Place to Begin 33

Introduction 33
Social Justice and Community 33
Social Engagement 34
Creativity and Alternative Learning Centers 34
Empowerment Theory and Peer Education 35
Community Art Education for Youth 'At Risk' 36
The Leave Out Violence Program 36
Westhaven-Elmhurst Community Recreation Association (WECRA) 38
Community-Engaged Learning with University Students 38
Conclusion 40

5 The Projects 42

Introduction 42
Prison Art Programs 42
Proposing Prison Programs 43
The Collective Voice – Producing a Prison Publication 44
Mentorship: LINC, EDGE, and Patrick (Pat) R. 47
In Retrospection … the Writing 48
Arts and Crafts versus Youth-driven Projects 51
The Creative Process and Imagery Selection 51
The Sunday Art + Design Group 53
The Mural Project 56

Indigenous Art and Design 58
The Outside Guide 58
A Pathway to Imagine and Build Spaces for Social Advocacy 61
Conclusion 61

6 Collaborative Projects 63

Introduction 63
Research Skills 63
Youth as Collaborators and Curriculum Builders 65

Postscript – Moving Forward 66

Appendices 69
Appendix A: A Reflective Letter by Patrick (Pat) R. 71
Appendix B: A Reflective Letter by Rafael Fuentes 75
Appendix C: A Reflective Letter by Tye S. 76

Part II: Peer-Support Workbook: Words from the Inside-Out 77

Index 137

Figures

5.1	*Inside-Out Magazine, A Retrospective*, cover top and credits	45
5.2	'Horror-scopes'	49
5.3	C.D., 'Tupac' drawing and wood burning	52
5.4	Anonymous, Self-Portrait, Pencil Drawing	53
5.5	Example of sock monkey project, Arts and Crafts Program	55
5.6	C.J. and C.R., Stages in painting mural on Unit 1	57
5.7	Background information for *The Outside Guide*	59
5.8	*The Outside Guide*, credit page	60
5.9	*The Outside Guide*, table of contents	60
6.1	Six of *The Outside Guide* researchers	64
6.2	Carol Cross and teens celebrate the completion of *The Outside Guide*	64

Preface

Justice-Involved Youth: Healing Through Trauma with Creativity and Community Regeneration + Peer-Support Workbook addresses the social implications of policies surrounding children and youth in care, paying particular attention to promoting a more humane deterrent to divert those 'at risk' or already justice-involved from entering (or re-entering) the criminal justice system, and offers a counter-narrative to current practices and policies. As a youth counselor supporting incarcerated male and female adolescents, I estimated that well over 75 per cent had experienced racism, poverty, emotional and/or physical abuse, and neglect. A high percentage had transitioned from foster care to incarceration.

Visual culture is an integral part of everyday lives and identities. Some forms of knowledge are more accessible while other are solely accessible through non-verbal means, and this can be specifically important when working with individuals affected by trauma and a history of violence, substance use disorder, homelessness, and gang affiliation. In a nationwide study, the prevalence of diagnosed disorders increased the further that youths were processed into the juvenile justice system (Wasserman et al., 2010).

Courts have tended to be conservative and legalistic in their interpretation of the law, giving little consideration to culturally sensitive assistance and the effects of intergenerational trauma. By looking into the social implications of policies surrounding children and adolescents in care, we draw attention to the need for promoting a more humane deterrent to divert those children and youth who are at risk of entering the criminal justice system.

With an emphasis on community partnerships, we introduce alternative ways of dealing with juvenile justice issues and promote a better understanding of those adolescents involved—a counter-narrative to restorative justice practices and policies. Sustainable community-based educational initiatives and partnerships can support, as well as interrupt, the cycle of violence. The importance of these community initiatives for 'at-risk' youth can increase their self-esteem, emotional wellbeing, and personal development. In this book, I offer readers an in-depth example of an after-school violence intervention program for at-risk youth that I started in Vancouver, British Columbia.

Adolescents have shared their lives, stories, and creativity in my programs. Throughout the following chapters, I introduce their voices, which can be identified in the text by use of italics. By sharing and reading the work of others, many of the adolescents involved expressed that they felt supported to get through difficult times in their lives. The *Peer-Support Workbook* in Part Two is a compilation of writing and art by participants. This project would not exist without their contributions.

By incorporating their visual art and stories, and surveying the literature on the criminal justice system and youth development theory, I shine light on young lives affected by a justice 'system' that enforces behavior modification in the name of rehabilitation; as well as on how punitive governance, predatory policing, surveillance, and mass incarceration impact the future of millions of our adolescents.

This project grew from my deep care and respect for adolescents who have experienced hardships, and/or have gotten into trouble with the law, and the value I found in implementing creativity when supporting and working with them. I have always found a great 'kid' behind a seemingly rough exterior. It is finding their hidden spirit, their potential, that sustains my belief in the value of the creative process of the arts as a catalyst for social activism and community spirit.

Finally, the transition of young people from youth and adult correctional facilities to society—a process termed youth re-entry—brings with it multiple challenges. It is my hope that this book will invite readers to continue to strive for concrete solutions on how best to effectively support and assist these youths.

Contact: carolcrossjiy@gmail.com

References

Wasserman, G.A., McReynolds, L.S., & Jones, S.A. (2010). Psychiatric disorder, comorbidity, & suicidal behavior in juvenile justice youth. *Criminal Justice and Behavior*, 37(2).

About the Thrive Collective

Featuring Art Direction by Chris 'Daze' Ellis (Brooklyn, 2016)

Thrive Collective creates hope and opportunity through arts, sports, and mentoring in and around public schools. Our core programs—Murals, Music, Media, Mentors, and Sports—connect artists, youth workers, and volunteers with local schools as teaching artists, art directors, coaches, and mentors. Project-based learning and accredited curriculum integrate life and art skills in four kinds of experiences: in-school electives, after school clubs, seasonal intensives, and weekend warriors. We incorporated in 2011 as a 501(c)(3) organization, and are a licensed New York vendor with numerous city agencies.

Since 2014, we have served 35,000 students in 250 schools, and worked in five states, as well as Washington DC, Puerto Rico, and Mexico. Together with 200 artists and 3500 volunteers from 120 partner organizations, our students have produced more than 600 murals exceeding 200,000 square feet of public art, 40 original songs and music videos, and nearly 100 student films.

In service,
Jeremy R. Del Rio, Esq.
Executive Director
Thrive

Chapter 1

Setting the Stage

Introduction

Visual culture is an integral part of everyday lives and identities. Many forms of knowledge are accessible only through non-verbal means. As a visual artist and expressive arts educator, I recognize the importance of art programs that go beyond the creation of art objects. There is an essential role for art as education and therapy, as well as unlimited potential for building collaborative partnerships that contribute to the strengthening of democratic communities. An important part of my role as an educator is to introduce new ideas or cultural tools where and when necessary, and then provide support and guidance for participants to make sense of these for themselves. We can then observe the ways in which the instructional activities are being interpreted and determine how best to modify or advance the activities to become more effective and warrant their continued engagement.

Research interests include exemplary social programs in non-traditional settings where a new educational orientation and dialogue can begin. The key point is that within these settings, community social service organizations have structures and ways of viewing youth as key assets, allowing them to create educational experiences and opportunities that empower young people. These organizations are transforming the way children and youth are *engaged* in and through the arts while promoting the value of creativity in lives. This is accomplished through helping participants discover their unique vision and responding to each as an individual who brings with them their own set of life experiences and beliefs, regardless of their age (McFee, 1998; hooks, 1995).

Using a contemporary, postmodernist curriculum, we can begin to challenge systems of domination that include class, racism, and sexism, providing an education that reaches out to a diverse group of participants. 'Constructivism' refers to the idea that each learner individually (and socially) constructs meaning as they learn. Constructivist learning theory dates back to American philosopher and educational reformer John Dewey (1916), whose ideas have been influential in both education and social policy. He believed that schools had to bring real world problems into the curriculum.

The psychologist Lev Vygotsky contributed to the idea that learning and development are internally tied to communicative interactions with others, and promoted learning contexts in which students played an *active* role in learning. The context in which a concept is taught, as well as participants' beliefs and attitudes, are important agents in the learning process.

The public schools of our nation remain the most obvious source for research on learning, though studies show that a growing number of education scholars are investigating life and learning beyond school as critical sites for youth development, cultural production,

DOI: 10.4324/9781003534082-1

and theory building (Heath, Soep, & Roach, 1998). They argue that artistic interventions and contemporary art programming have the capacity to address issues relevant to today's society. As Michel Foucault (1980) wrote: 'What strikes me is the fact that in our society, art has become something that is only related to objects, and not to individuals or to life.'

Traumatic experience can disrupt the ability of children to learn/process verbal information and use language as a vehicle for communication. These language problems can undermine literacy skills, social-emotional development and behavioral regulation, and can also adversely affect the ability to have good peer and adult relationships (DeBellis, 2005, p. 61). The process of being institutionalized as an adolescent is itself traumatic—receiving discipline instead of treatment, and then being diagnosed as having a conduct disorder. Lacking the words to communicate their pain, these young people may express feelings of vulnerability by becoming aggressive or feigning disinterest in academic success because they believe they cannot succeed.

Trauma and Healing through Creative Expression

Morrison (2009) speaks to the importance of writing as meaningful and relevant: 'Certain kinds of trauma visited on peoples are so deep, so cruel, that unlike money, unlike vengeance, even unlike justice, or rights, or the goodwill of others, only writers can translate such trauma and turn sorrow into meaning sharpening the moral imagination' (p. 4).

Trauma can be physical or psychological, the result of an accident, war, illness, bullying or other types of abuse, and may be something that has happened in the past—but the body will keep reacting as if in imminent danger, and 'triggers' can arise at any time. More specifically, if life histories are not taken into consideration, and psychological and personal issues stemming from childhood experiences are not addressed and instead denied, the chance to express and work through grief, frustrations, and other feelings can impede, and sometimes halt, a healthy and natural process of identity formation. Some youth will 'shut down' not wanting to relive a history of personal trauma—this can result in delinquency through trauma, and transition to poor choices as adults.

As a counselor with juvenile offenders, I was surprised to find that some adolescents were not able to read or write well (if at all). I decided to offer teens on intake a small journal that they could keep with them. In my practice, I believe that drawing can be a way to get in contact with silent or wordless knowledge—another kind of intuitive thinking than the logical/verbal. The young people I worked with would sometimes bring their journals to a next meeting. Although society urges us to make choices in life based on logic, the *intuitive* way of thinking can help us to understand and maybe solve our problems.

Cognitive Conflict

Cognitive conflict is a normal part of growth. Many developmental psychologists argue that children overcome cognitive conflict through internal processes of assimilation and accommodation—this is how they come to understand the nature of the world and their place in it. Jean Piaget believed that human beings inherit two basic tendencies: *organization* (the tendency to systemize and combine processes into coherent general systems) and *adaptation* (the tendency to adjust to the environment). In Piaget's view, adolescents from the ages of 12 to 18 years will adapt by *assimilation* (interpreting an experience so that it fits an existing scheme), or by *accommodation* (changing an existing scheme to incorporate the experience) (Snowman & Biehler, 2006). Adolescents entering a correctional institution have little choice but to learn to adapt to the many restrictions they will be subjected to in this environment. Programs should be made available that prevent the transition from juvenile delinquency to young adult offending. Intensive probation or parole has been found to be moderately effective, while restorative and reparative programs were quite effective. The most effective programs were skill building and counseling programs such as mentoring (Lipsey, 2009, pp. 124–147).

While art speaks to our *need* to heal, can it actually *facilitate* healing for those who create it, and for those who view it? In her essay, 'Up the revolution', performance artist Linda Burnham, writes about the interaction between 'non-artists and art-world refugees': 'They are making art, not therapy … though the results are undeniably therapeutic' (Burnham & Durland, 1989, p. 12). Artistic works are always *about* something: they have meanings to interpret and can be about social or personal issues (Parsons, 1992). Reflecting on my professional experience, I found the use of the creative arts to be a means to foster individual growth and healing.

A teen participant, J.D., wrote that writing helped him '*… vent my frustrations by writing down my feelings and it keeps me off the streets, after 13 years of psychiatric treatment, 5 years in detention, and 3 months in a psychiatric hospital …*'

Democracy and Creativity

Mansbridge (1991) suggests that democracy involves public discussion of common problems. She also claims that certain groups sometimes cannot find the right voice or words to express their thoughts, and when they do, they discover that they are not heard. Giroux (2003) states that youth, as a complex, shifting and contradictory category, are rarely narrated in the dominant public sphere through their diverse voices. If we are a 'democratic' society, every one of us, regardless of our history, should have the help we need in order to re-engage within society. Emotional wellbeing needs to be viewed as a vital part of our overall health. The creative arts are an essential component in the healing process. Patrick (Pat) R. explains that his involvement with writing:

> *… had begun several years earlier when a psychologist at the Regional Health Centre, a special needs prison that provides extensive programs for violent offenders, suggested that I take up writing to better understand and express my emotions, something I always had trouble doing and subsequently often got me in trouble … writing not only helped me understand and express my emotions, but more importantly, it helped me understand some of the complicated social issues that culminated in me taking another man's life …*
>
> (see Appendix A for Pat's complete letter about the importance of art in correctional institutions).

Resiliency and Recovery

A study of 'high risk' youth followed into adulthood found a significant degree of resilience and recovery over time, due in large part to more adult support to help these youth develop emotional resiliency and coping skills. Many had faced multiple and interacting risks in their families, communities, peer worlds, and school environments. The study also found that maltreated children were more likely than non-maltreated children to engage in aggressive behaviors, as well as experience attention deficits and emotional deregulation. Physically abused children were at risk for reactive aggression, and if not prevented or treated early, were likely to grow up to lead traumatized and traumatizing lives.

A report studying facilities across Canada found that 57 per cent of young offenders had a connection to the child welfare system. In British Columbia, where I live, that number rose to 73 per cent. Another problem was the lack of mental health support. Children's mental health centers in the country were (and still are) facing some very long waiting lists, and child welfare clients, even though they are children who are wards of the state, often do not get to the top of these lists. (Information retrieved March 26, 2007 from www.prisonjustice.ca).

The report also addressed a system that is penalizing youth for their background and moving them into the youth justice system where it will be very difficult for them to be successful during the rest of their lives. They have complex needs that need special care and special programming to succeed.

Trauma can take our voices away. Exposure to violence can alter not only how we see the world, but also how we see others and perceive our own worth. Violent conduct ranks among the types of inappropriate behavior generally originating in difficult family and social contexts. Providing a safe space—both physically and psychologically—and by devising new and creative prevention and intervention methods, we can integrate mental health supports for those children and adolescents who are designated 'at-risk'.

Yoga, theater, and art programs are important activities that can help reduce hyperarousal, and help them focus and learn.

Discussing the impact of trauma on one's worldview, Judith Herman, states that recovery from trauma 'follows a common pathway'. The fundamental stages of recovery are establishing safety, reconstructing the trauma story, and restoring the connection between survivors and their community. Traumatic events destroy the victim's fundamental assumptions about the safety of the world, the positive value of the self, and the meaningful order of creation (Herman, 1997). Creativity can provide the chance to express and work through grief, frustration, and other feelings. We can accomplish this by providing a safe environment where participants feel valued for their experiences and opinions, and somewhere where they can *freely* express feelings and emotions that are important to them.

Traditional intervention strategies, such as special education, school counseling and guidance, are not sufficient—schools typically close at three in the afternoon. In lieu of expelling or suspension for inappropriate behavior, students should be receiving additional support. School-based intervention programs can help to support resiliency in at-risk adolescents (Noam, 1996). In 2000, I was contracted to set up a non-profit, after-school program for teens 'at risk' in Vancouver, Canada. Leave Out Violence has a mandate to assist young people whose lives have been affected by violence. My involvement with this project provided me with the opportunity to advance a cause I feel strongly about—violence prevention—and to engage with teens in seeking arts-based solutions to social problems.

The Leave Out Violence program, introduced in Chapter 4, engaged the involved teens in pro-social activities that involved two things: 1) peer education, and 2) youth-driven activities. I have foregrounded these criteria because the programs I have been involved in during my professional life—programs such as Leave out Violence—owe their success in large part to these essential pillars.

Trauma and Suicide

Neglect and abuse primes us to seek other ways to meet our needs. In an issue of *The New Yorker* (April 4, 2022), an article appeared, titled 'The mystifying rise of child suicide, A family tragedy sheds light on a burgeoning mental-health emergency'. Andrew Solomon

(2022) reports that child suicide takes place more often during the school year when social and academic stresses are highest. Bullying was strongly associated with suicide not only among its victims but also among its perpetrators—'Children's worlds may be smaller than adults, but their emotional horizons are just as wide.'

According to a study published in the *Journal of Adolescent Health*, by the age of 13, more than a third of bullies considered ending their lives. In Canada, a Youth Risk Behavior Survey (2017), found that suicide is the second highest cause of death for 10–24-year-olds (Retrieved April 6, 2022 from https://canadiancrc.com/Youth_Suicide_in_canada.aspx).

Non-suicidal self-injury (NSSI) is the 'intentional destruction of one's own body tissue without suicidal intent, and for purposes not socially sanctioned' (Klonsky, Victor, & Saffer, 2014).

A coping mechanism for some of the adolescents I worked with (in detention and in community), included behaviors such as carving, cutting, or burning oneself; banging or punching objects or oneself; and embedding objects under the skin. According to a U.S. study, approximately 15–20 per cent of adolescents and young adults engage in self-injury at least once. Tattooing and piercings are not considered NSSI because they are seen to be culturally sanctioned forms of expression.

Personal histories of childhood (physical or sexual) abuse, as well as parental neglect and separations, have been associated with risk factors for suicide attempts and a variety of self-destructive behaviors into adulthood (Lopez-Castroman & Courtet, 2014).

Pharmacological Treatment and Young Offenders

Upon intake, a high percentage of incarcerated teens told me they were on, or had often been prescribed, anti-psychotics, such as Seroquel, Concerta, and Lithium, to modify behavior. Ritalin was generally prescribed for ADHD. Although I was unable to uncover any internal documents reporting the exact percentage of teens prescribed 'meds' while in custody, Currie (2004) adds: '... by the time they reached high school, if not before, many were already veteran consumers of a bewildering variety of pharmaceutical drugs' (p. 129). He states that the majority of positive studies on medications reviewed were sponsored by pharmaceutical companies, and either had exaggerated the benefits, downplayed the harms, or both. (p. 138).

Despite a report by the American Psychological Association (APA), that *all* psychotropic drugs have the potential for cognitive toxicity, a high percentage of the teens I met at the correctional facility, were, or had often been prescribed some form of medication. Depression, anxiety, fetal alcohol syndrome, and other conditions, can best be served by multiple methodologies, and not that of buying into a medical model of health care that pathologizes, in lieu of dealing with the social welfare of those disadvantaged youth. Traumatized children and adolescents need alternate ways to deal with these issues, and if prescribed pharmaceutical drugs are found to be necessary, those taking them should be closely monitored for side effects and other long-term health hazards.

Why Art Matters

Giroux (2003) states that youth, as a complex, shifting, and contradictory category, are rarely narrated in the dominant public sphere through their diverse voices. Constance Bumgarner Gee (2004) points to the many assertions about the capacity of the arts to assist in spiritual and moral development, improve academic performance, and induce psychological and even physiological wellbeing. Bumgarner Gee (1996) cites Champions of Change as an example, promoting seven arts intervention projects as 'models of excellence'. The report included *non-school projects* that focus entirely on local artists and arts groups to provide services outside of the school setting. In a later and more comprehensive report, *Champions of Change: The impact of the arts on learning*, many independent researchers found that engagement in the arts nurtures the development of cognitive skills, as well as social and personal competencies, thereby improving youth's attitudes about themselves and decreasing youth involvement in delinquent behavior (Americans for the Arts, 1999).

Let's remember that for most of us, as children, we were rewarded when we brought home that drawing or craft made at school. It was usually pinned on the wall or positioned on the fridge door, given as a present to a relative, or put on a mantelpiece as a trophy. But while these drawings and crafts may be admired, they are not really understood; parents and even teachers tend to overlook the developmental importance of these creative achievements. As children enter adolescence, artistic creativity wanes; artistic learning is marginalized and trivialized as akin to a hobby and not something that is necessary. Schools claim to require more time for learning 'core subjects' of language arts, mathematics, and sciences. Exploration with art materials is often dismissed as 'mere play' rather than serious work. There are many anecdotal reports of arts-emphasis teaching including testimonials about the benefits that accrue to education when we capitalize on the interests and capabilities of developing a dialogue of issues pertaining to the individual and society—topics of interest to young people, and their need to feel a sense of mastery of themselves.

In a custodial setting, helping teens resolve conflicts and disagreements peacefully can help improve socializing, particularly in regards to group situations. In his book, *Social Intelligence: The new science of human relationships*, Daniel Goleman (2006) writes, 'Psychologists argue about which human abilities are social and which are emotional' (p. 82). Simply put, it is through how we interact with others in social situations, particularly 'in turbulent social currents', that social intelligence can help the adolescent transform a potentially hostile situation into a positive outcome.

Collaborative art programs can develop social intelligence—teens socialize with peers and learn not to compete with one another, instead collaborating in order to obtain shared results. Most importantly, collaborating on projects with incarcerated teens offers a positive experience to help them regain what the institutional system and the circumstances of their lives sometimes obliterate—a sense of individual identity and confidence in human interaction.

Personal Healing and Creativity

Justice-involved youths need to reflect on current elements of their everyday experiences in a safe and supportive environment, and address issues relevant to their subculture.

Creative projects can promote psychological and spiritual wellness, and I have always included creative projects when working with individuals. Unlike traditional arts and crafts programs, the *process* of creation is emphasized rather than the final product. In my role as a correctional facility's youth counselor, I was there to support young people while incarcerated and beyond—with some continuing to keep in touch on the 'outs'.

Adolescents need to feel they can share what they have written without fear of ridicule. We reaffirm our uniqueness by tapping into creativity and incorporating our own story as a starting point. There is a difference between using *personal* experiences as a starting point for a story as opposed to one that has been previously published. In the after-school community program of Tim Rollins and K.O.S. (Kids of Survival) in New York, youth attempt to identify with the protagonist—the 'other'. I point this out, not to diminish the successful work of K.O.S., but to mention my findings. When youths develop their own story, as in the Leave Out Violence program, they control their storytelling—there is not always a beginning, middle, and an end. They took ownership, built self-esteem, and in a sense, uncovered a talent within. The process of embodying a story in a creative and safe space, allowed them to discover what they already possess—an imagination, and a natural and unique way of expressing it. And I listened to their concerns regarding the lack of materials available for any kind of expressive mediums in their schools, and a need for a safe place to turn to, to get a handle on their lives—the tragedies and the stories. Programs can provide both engaging and invigorating ways of learning by developing individuality and confidence through creative activities, encouraging a sense of belonging.

Incarcerated teens can feel estranged from the world and need guidance to channel their personal history. They need support and opportunities to share their ideas and life experiences in a safe space that can encourage literacy, self-expression, and critical thinking skills. The creative arts can provide the imprisoned with a voice. This can result in powerful, emotionally charged works of art, as in the following excerpt of reflective writing. O. shares with readers how her life is affected by her family's struggle with drug and alcohol addictions:

> *One mother, one father, but they never do stay. A mommy, a daddy, but Mommy's gone away. A mamma, a papa, but Daddy's left again. A mom and a dad but I've never known them together. And mamma ran away long ago, it really is too bad. Who's fighting the drug war? Daddy couldn't stand to watch my sisters ruin themselves each day. With all the crack and heroin there was no other way. Mommy, well I can't even begin to begin with her. She sold her soul to the devil, sold it away for sure. I never knew her not to be drunk. While she told me she loved me, well she never really did care. Yes, she was in my life, but she was never really there. She's always been a-running and forever been a-shunning. Well yes, I've got two parents, but they've never been around. I've come to accept it all and smile through my frown.*

In O's poignant story, she steps back to gain perspective and realizes her own parents are 'damaged'. Perhaps this realization, that she and her siblings have suffered in different ways and different degrees, has enabled her to experience a therapeutic moment of acceptance and an ability to 'smile through my frown'.

Conclusion

A draft report developed by the National Symposium on Art Education (2001) advocates for the arts in engaging with others in personal healing and learning: 'We also live in a time when violence and misunderstandings seem to be spreading in our society. The arts can be a direct way of vicariously but meaningfully encountering sensitive issues and values' (pp. 4–5). This is especially important for children and adolescents who have experienced trauma and/or feel left out of mainstream society. 'Regardless of subject matter, form, or content, whether art is political or not ... art [allows for] freedom of expression ... a place where boundaries can be transgressed ...' (hooks, 1995, p. 138).

Art is connected to social change. Creative projects offer a place to share opinions and generate solutions; and in this context, the arts become participatory democracy in action, even in places that are not necessarily seen as democratic spaces. Through encouragement, proper instruction, and with artistic tools made available, creative expression can flourish, allowing for an opportunity to create work that is fearless, fresh, and innovative even in a prison environment.

Chapter 2 will continue the discussion of helping adolescents with the management of issues, such as affect regulation, altered relationships with themselves and others, and the influence of programming in the context of working with justice-involved youth. The shift in the focus of learning is no longer on the individual alone but on the individual *interacting* within a larger socio-cultural context.

References

Americans for the Arts (1999). Champions of Change: The impact of the arts on learning. Retrieved February 1, 2007, from https://www.americansforthe arts.org/information_services/arts_educ_communityresource_center_007.asp.

Bumgarner Gee, C.M. (1996). President's Committee on the Art and Humanities & the Arts Education Partnership, Champions of Change Inc., Rochester, New York. Retrieved January 1, 1998 from http://championsofchange.org.

Bumgarner Gee, C.M. (2004). Spirit, mind, and body: Arts education the redeemer. In E. Eisner & M. Day (Eds.) *Handbook of Research and Policy in Art Education*. Reprinted in *Arts Education Policy Review*, March/April 2004.

Burnham, L.F. & Durland, S. (Eds.) (1989). *The Citizen Artist: 20 years of art in the public area: An anthology from High Performance Magazine 1978–1998. Vol 1. Thinking Publicly: The new era of public art*. Gardiner, N.Y.: Critical Press.

Currie, E. (2004). *The Road to Whatever*. New York: Henry Holt.

DeBellis, M.D. (2005). The psychbiology of neglect. *Child Maltreatment*, 10(2).

Dewey, J. (1916). *Democracy and Education*. New York: Free Press.

Ellsworth, E. (1989). Why doesn't this feel empowering? Working through the repressive myths of critical pedagogy. *Harvard Educational Review*, 59(3), 297–324.

Foucault, M. (1980). *Power/Knowledge: Selected interviews and other writings, 1972–1977*. New York: Pantheon.

Giroux, H.A. (2003). Public pedagogy and the politics of resistance: Notes on a critical theory of educational struggle. *Educational Philosophy & Theory*, 35, 5–16.

Goleman, D. (2006). *Social Intelligence: The new science of human relationships*. New York: Random House.

Heath, S.B., Soep, E., & Roach, A. (1998). Living the arts through language-learning: A report on community-based youth organizations. *Americans for the Arts, Monographs*, 2.

Herman, I. (1997). *Trauma and Recovery*. New York: Basic Books.

hooks, b. (1995). *Art on My Mind: Visual politics*. New York: The New Press.

Klonsky, E.D., Victor, S.E., & Saffer, B.Y. (2014). Non-suicidal self-injury: What we know and what we need to know. *Canadian Journal of Psychiatry*, 59(11), 565–568.

Lipsey, M.W. (2009). *The primary factors that characterize effective interventions with juvenile offenders: A meta-analytic overview* (pp. 124–127). New York: Taylor & Francis.

Lopez-Castroman, J. & Courtet, P. (2014). The additive effect on suicidality of family history of suicidal behavior and early traumatic experiences. Retrieved September 11, 2024 from Archives of Suicide Research, www.academia.edu/22652988.

McFee, J.K. (1998). *Cultural Diversity and the Structure and Practice of Art Education*. Reston, VA: National Art Education Association.

Mansbridge, J. (1991). Democracy, deliberation, and the experience of women. In B. Murchland (Ed.), *Higher education and the practice of democratic politics: A political education reader* (pp. 122–135). Dayton, OH: Kettering Foundation.
Morrison, T. (2009). Peril. In T. Morrison (Ed.) *Burn this Book: Notes on literature and engagement* (p. 4). New York: Harper Collins.
National Symposium on Art Education (2001, July). *Sharing the Vision: A national framework for arts education in Canadian schools*. Symposium conducted at Calgary, AB, Canada.
Noam, G.G. (1996). The Harvard rally program and the prevention practitioner: Comprehensive, school-based intervention to support resiliency in at-risk adolescents. *Journal of Child and Youth Care Work*, 11, 32–47.
Parsons, M. (1992). Cognition as interpretation in art education. In B. Reimer & R.A. Smith (Eds.) *The Arts, Education, and Aesthetic Knowing* (pp. 70–91). Chicago, IL: The National Society for the Study of Education.
Snowman, H., & Biehler, R. (2006). *Psychology Applied to Teaching*. Belmont, CA: Wadsworth Publishing.
Solomon, A. (2022). The mystifying rise of child suicide. *The New Yorker*, April 4, 2022.
Solomon, R.C. (2002). Back to basics: on the very idea of 'basic emotions'. *Journal for the Theory of Social Behavior*, 32(2), 115–144.
Vygotsky, L.S. (1978). Interaction between learning and development. In M. Gauvain & M. Cole (Eds.) *Readings on the Development of Children*. New York: Scientific American Books.

Chapter 2

Social Justice

Shifting Powers

Introduction

Social justice is the view that everyone deserves economic, political, and social rights and opportunities. The five main aims of social justice are: access to resources, equity, participation, diversity, and human rights (see www.ojp.gov).

This chapter discusses the shift to a more compassionate and effective way of recognizing and healing the impacts of trauma, and is drawn from my understanding of the use of creativity to heal and improve emotional states and behavior. Art is connected to social change and is a fundamental human activity. The expressive arts lay groundwork for change. The shift is the focus of learning is no longer the individual alone, but the individual *interacting* within a cultural context. This acknowledges the cognitive capacities that inform artistic making and thinking.

Reform and Advocacy: Post Traumatic Stress Disorder (PTSD)

Reactive aggression and post-traumatic stress disorder are affected by violence. This can result from a family history of physical, psychological, and/or sexual abuse. Symptoms can occur as the result of exposure to violence (experiencing or witnessing abuse). Violence can also continue while incarcerated. Studies have found that youth who become involved in the juvenile justice system are several times more likely than other youth to have suffered trauma or adverse childhood experiences while growing up.

It is important to understand a youth's often troubled past. Statistics obtained through the Massachusetts Youth Screening Instrument-2 (MAYSI-2) reported that of the 730 teens I interviewed on intake, 80 per cent reported previous incarceration, and 72 per cent reported having seen a therapist (mental health practitioner such as a psychologist, psychiatrist, family and/or school counselor). The many "'repeat offenders"'I encountered at the correctional facility had personal histories of abuse and neglect; therefore, in my view, it makes little ethical sense to continue this pattern of abuse and punishment through legal sanctions.

C.J. shared an early childhood memory of parental neglect:

> *My earliest memory of my sister and I—there was no food and we were hungry. We walked out of the house and crawled under a fence and approached some construction workers. We sat beside them while they were eating their sandwiches and that's how we got to eat ...*
>
> (personal communication, 2008)

DOI: 10.4324/9781003534082-2

Wellbeing and the Expressive Arts

Wilcock (1998) describes wellbeing as a 'subjective assessment of health which is less concerned with biological functions than with feelings such as self-esteem and a sense of belonging through social integration' (p. 8).

> Their stories reflect the core of their experiences. Story of choices ... big and small that can lead us from trauma to triumph, from darkness to light, from imprisonment to freedom. Change is about noticing what's no longer working and stepping out of the familiar, imprisoning patterns. Anything we practice we become more good at it. If we practice anger, we'll have more anger. If we practice fear, we'll have more fear. In many cases, we actually work very hard to ensure that we go nowhere.
>
> (Evan-Egar, 2017)

Kelly (cited in Silverstein, 1973) states that youth and the creation of art emerges as a philosophy of approach when developing holistic health services for young people and is derived from values found in youth-driven community art programs. Introducing youth-driven programs follows what Efland refers to as an expressionist stream that believes 'art can be a vehicle to express emotions by accessing the unconscious resulting in positive developmental growth' (cited in Siegesmund, 1998). Through the therapeutic benefits of art, mental health is fostered and participants can safely experience emotions through their 'imaginative projections' (Siegesmund, 1998, p. 201). Applying this to my work with incarcerated teens showed me that participants involved in youth-driven projects appreciated the opportunity for the freedom of personal and creative expression, subsequently fostering their emotional wellbeing, and this provided a vehicle for them to express traumatic past experiences. Some common themes in creative writing were: emotional hurt; making wrong choices; searching for a sense of identity and 'belonging'; and the need for, but lack of mentors and/or parental guidance, and unconditional love.

Our own personal lives and professional experiences may provide our material, but by listening to *their* stories, as the poet and writer Grady Hillman, who has worked in over 50 adult and juvenile correctional facilities, so perfectly puts it, you learn about both the potential and the tragedy of the human condition, and that's the stuff of art.

Whereas language is abstract, we need to broaden our definition of the term 'art', and the way we approach it, value it, and educate others with and through it. The following is an example of K. sharing a personal tragedy—the loss of a close friend and his feelings of hopelessness for lives filled with emotional and physical abuse. In all my years working with teens, I had never witnessed a young person who had self-mutilated his body so severely. Highly artistic and intelligent, I always looked forward to our meetings, and I believe that projects such as *Inside-Out Magazine*, introduced in Chapter 5, provided a forum for teens like K. to write about childhood trauma in the form of abuses and/or loss, including the reality of individuals who self-mutilate to deal with internalized anger, as well as a positive outlet to express and share these emotions. His excerpt below, 'Crimson Tears', shares memories of finding his girlfriend dead and resorting to self-harm to relieve his emotional pain.

> *Crimson Tears caress my face, blood drips down my arm, slice, slice, slice, my little game of self-harm. There is nothing left. No more life means no more pain. Then I found you in all your grace, just lying there with a smirk on your face. A ring of crimson circles around you, on the floor lays a dull black .22. Now you're dead at 16 years. I sit on the floor alone crying my crimson tears.*

The Link between Childhood Experience and Delinquency

> Prisons do not disappear problems, they disappear human beings.
>
> Angela Davis

In all of the four correctional units, I worked with a wide mix of teens according to their ages and the length and type of sentences received, including perpetrators and/or survivors of traumatic experiences and those suffering a history of aggression, violence, neglect, and abuse.

In a study of British youth who committed violent offences (Kurtz, Thornes, & Bailey, 1998), it was noted that an astonishing 91 per cent had experienced childhood trauma in the form of abuse and/or loss, and frequently both. The researchers suggest the rate of mental health disorder is high in young offenders, particularly *persistent* offenders. Adverse childhood experience and disturbed and delinquent behavior are linked with family history. 'Young offenders usually come from homes characterized by: neglect, abuse and a lack of supervision and parental involvement, together with inadequate and inconsistent discipline, conflict, parental criminal behaviors and attitudes that condone law-breaking' (Kurtz, Thornes, & Bailey, p. 544). The study's authors conclude that unless the specific problems of each teen are identified and expertly assessed with appropriate interventions made available, 'young offender institutions remain expensive placements that will achieve little other than containment' (p. 551).

Young people need to develop a healthy self-identity; without that, healthy coping habits are near impossible to achieve. In Canada, youth aged 14 or older can be sentenced as adults, but the decision is made only after the accused has been found guilty in a youth court. If sentenced as an adult, the juvenile (aged 12–17) will remain incarcerated in a juvenile facility until the age of 18, and then transferred to an adult prison. In my professional experience, this depended on the clinical team, and in rare cases youth finished their sentence in a youth facility at the age of 21 (a young adult in Canada is between the ages of 18–24). Upon intake, teens reported that they had been, or were being counseled by someone in the mental health profession.

They also often reported feeling that they did not find a sympathetic ear nor did they think their account of events was understood or believed by these adults. Sometimes there is shame associated with the criminal behavior—we need to look at the person beneath the label of 'young offender'. On intake, I also let them know that no matter what their criminal charges, I was there to support them to the best of my ability.

Susan Kools (1997), examined the impact that foster care has on adolescents. She found that very few researchers have interviewed children in foster care to explore their thoughts and feelings about their status as foster children or their placement experiences. She further states that most theoretical and empirical literature on *normative* child and adolescent development places the developing child within the context of the *family* system. Investigators have begun to gather evidence that 'severe functional impairment is suffered by children in foster care as a group, including poor academic achievement, behavioral and emotional problems, and health-related problems' (p. 263). It would then make sense to conclude that the adolescents' expectations for their future are reduced and adjusted accordingly.

A term society commonly uses to refer to these teens is 'troubled', although I believe it is their lives that are 'troubled,' not them. Indeed, many have experienced racism, poverty, emotional or physical abuse, and neglect while in care; others have suffered the loss of one of both parents. Even the small percentage living with families speak of surviving some form of familial neglect. They face yet another life challenge when they enter a correctional facility.

Intergenerational Trauma

We should take into account, when working with our Indigenous youths, the impact that intergenerational trauma can have on their lives. The correctional facility I was involved with contracted an Elder who visited with youths. She also provided specific programming to meet their needs.

Generational trauma occurs when the impact of a traumatic event is not limited to the person who has directly experienced the trauma, but can influence their children, grandchildren, and even their community. Researchers have recognized that the healing of intergenerational trauma must include the family and the community. Traditional healing practices can include healing circles, sweat lodges, fasting, vision quest, and other ceremonies (Menzies, 2008). Although these findings have strong applicability for our Aboriginal young offender populations and the Department of Justice Canada has provided several important areas of scientific inquiry, further research is needed as a significant gap currently exists (see http://www.justice.gc.ca, Government of Canada Publications, Youth Justice Research, retrieved January 13, 2025).

A survey conducted by The McCreary Centre Society (2002) reported that youth (137 took part in their survey), spoke about the difficulties of being released from custody and how they often felt confused—'false preparation happens a lot, you forget what life is like on the outs.' When asked how to improve the release planning process, one youth said, 'people should actually listen to what we say and not presume they know what we want' (2002, p. 25). The document, which can be downloaded from the McCreary website (www.mcs.bc.ca, retrieved January 13, 2025), reported that teens suggested the implementation of youth-run programs and expressed interest in peer-led activities and greater involvement in custody center life. Youth recommendations included:

- Youth-run conferences in the centers in which residents learn how to organize and present workshops for other youth.
- Programming where youth choose the programs they participate in and help to plan their own activities.

The McCreary Centre Society's report included photographs showcasing four murals we had completed, with the simple caption 'mural painted by youth.'

The Youth Criminal Justice Act – Canada

Contrary to public perception of the juvenile justice system as lenient, the seriousness of youth dispositions has increased. Prior to the inception in 2003 of the Youth Criminal Justice Act, Canada jailed young people at four times the rate at which it incarcerated adults; and, 10–-15 times the incarceration rate of European countries.

The aims of the Youth Criminal Justice Act (YCJA) are:

1 To carry out the orders of the court.
2 To protect society by providing supervision and interventions in a safe and supportive environment.
3 To facilitate rehabilitation by providing youth with optimal opportunities for healthy growth and pro-social development through: effective programs that respond to the individual and cultural needs of youth; a youth-focused integrated case management process that provides for comprehensive and dynamic case plans; and implementing strategies that promote successful reintegration to the community.

(Ministry of Children and Family Development, Youth Justice Policy and Program Support, internal document, 2005, p. 1b)

Youth justice policies need to apply restorative justice practices as the primary model for dealing with wrongdoing and conflict, as well as emphasizing the psychological value of healing and treatment approaches. The more punitive approach I witnessed being practiced seemed ineffective to me. The punishment model is based on the theory that punitive measures are the most effective way to reform or rehabilitate youth to make their reintegration into society easier. Although young people should be held responsible for their behavior, they nevertheless have special needs that may require alternative efforts at rehabilitation.

The Youth Criminal Justice Act does include provision for an Intensive Rehabilitative Custody and Supervision (IRCS) Order. This option is considered as an *alternative to an adult sentence* and is available if the provincial director has determined that an IRCS program is appropriate as a plan of treatment (1) to reduce the risk of the young offender repeating one of the following categories of offences: murder, attempted murder, manslaughter, or aggravated sexual assault; or (2) the youth suffers from a mental illness or disorder, a psychological disorder, or an emotional disturbance. IRCS agreements require intensive planning on the part of the Ministry of Children and Family Development, Youth Forensics, the teen's lawyer, and their probation officer. Under the IRCS order, a teen could be provided with approximately $110,000 to be used for rehabilitation. They must agree to follow through with the course of treatment outlined by the custody center's clinical team or, their psychologist and/or psychiatrist, but during my years as the youths' counselor, only two males accepted an IRCS agreement.

Fetal Alcohol Syndrome Disorder (FASD)

Fetal Alcohol Syndrome Disorder (FASD) is an umbrella term used to describe a number of conditions. As noted below, most of these behaviors are a direct result of brain damage.

A paper prepared for the Canadian Ministry of Children and Family Development, by probation officer Frank Morven, in consultation with researcher and academic Dr. Andrea Scarth, reads as follows:

> The inappropriate behavior of individuals with FASD is often misinterpreted as being willful, volitional, or intentional. With this belief, the result is most often punishment, which in turn can result in an array of secondary defensive behaviors such as anger, school failure, mental health problems, running away, and trouble with the law. These somewhat secondary behaviors are somewhat preventable by reframing perceptions and

> providing support. We need to shift from seeing an individual as one who *won't* to seeing an individual as one who *can't*. Without understanding the impact of FASD, many Probation Officers may think the affected person is being 'difficult' rather than being unable to process and remember information. Those affected by FASD are all different ... [their] ability to understand the legal process, and to act as a witness on their own behalf, may be compromised due to weak memory and poor ability to understand and communicate. The concepts of 'intent', 'protection of the public' and 'rehabilitation' needs to be evaluated with the knowledge of disabilities associated with FASD.
>
> (Fetal Alcohol Spectrum Disorder (FASD)/Frank Morven/internal document, date unknown)

It concludes that some of the behaviors that are labeled 'criminal' are symptoms that are better treated therapeutically rather than punitively. However, these findings were *not* included in the Youth Criminal Justice Act document.

> C.B.'s name came up tonight. B. was emotionally moved by C. presenting his life's story in our group counseling session tonight. C. is a suicide risk—he's tried 3 times already and all 3 times he had a friend that we called 'an angel' stop him. I fear if he starts drinking again and gets depressed he'll try again—he might become one more teen suicide statistic. He can barely print and was diagnosed FASD.
>
> (Carol Cross, journal entry, September 29, 2005)

In an issue of *The Globe and Mail* (January 30, 2010), an article appeared titled, 'Fetal Alcohol Spectrum Disorder: Motor-skill activities hold promise of rewiring children's damaged brains.' Chris Bertram (2010), a scientist at the University of the Fraser Valley in Abbotsford, BC, investigated whether children with FASD 'can rewire their brains by improving their strongest motor skills.' He said that many of the current therapies or interventions used focus on their deficits—for example, anger management therapy for a child who is acting out in school, or extra time devoted to reading or math for a child struggling with those subjects.

'Traditional intervention programs have these kids doing things their brains are not adept at doing,' he explained 'and their success rates are not great. We flipped things around and said, "Why don't we build intervention programs based on things they're good at." (2010, p. A12)

BIPOC (Black, Indigenous, People of Color) and Culturally-Sensitive Support

I use the term as a way to reclaim oppressive labels given to racially marginalized groups. Imprisoned adolescents are essentially 'invisible' in this respect but in other respects they are very visible and often regarded as threatening to others. An observation by 17-year old Jason, typifies this view:

> If you had a problem in the Black community, and you brought in a group of White people to discuss how to solve it ... there'd probably be a public outcry. But every day, in local arenas all the way to the White House, adults sit around and decide what problems youth have and what youth need, without ever consulting us.
>
> (Delgado, 2006, p. 31)

'Aboriginal', a legal term recognized in the Canadian Constitution, recognizes three groups of Indigenous peoples: First Nations, Inuit, and Metis. There can be dozens of reserves within treaty boundaries—there are 32 different bands on Vancouver Island in British Columbia, Canada. This differs from the United States where reservations generally cover an entire treaty area.

The Youth Criminal Justice Act document includes criteria to limit the use of custody for all young persons. In addition, the act requires that all available options other than custody be considered during sentencing '... with particular attention to the circumstances of Aboriginal young persons with special requirements' (p.2). The document also revealed that 69 per cent of Aboriginal youth in custody reported having been told by a health professional that they had one or more health conditions or disabilities such as chronic anxiety, depression, addictions, attention deficit hyperactivity disorder (ADHD) and other learning disabilities including those associated with Fetal Alcohol Spectrum Disorders (FASD) (cited in YCJA, p. 2).

The literature, although sparse, does provide some preliminary evidence for the provision of culturally specific treatment services. Correctional Services Canada reported on federal Aboriginal offenders admitted to Healing Lodge programs, and found that almost 70 per cent of the clients completed the programs. In addition, and arguably more importantly, only 6 per cent of program clients returned to custody, a statistic which is even more impressive when one considers that the national average is 12 per cent (Wilson, 2000). Further evidence regarding the importance of culturally specific treatment is obtained from the work of Waldram (1994) who found promising evidence for Aboriginal spirituality using a case study approach. Research conducted in New Zealand also found lower rates of reoffending among Maori offenders who reported *cultural pride* and *cultural knowledge.*

The Nelson Mandela Rules

The United Nations' Nelson Mandela Rules outline the minimum standards for the treatment of prisoners and conditions of detention, and offer essential practical guidance to prison administrators. However, findings show a reluctance to adhere to their recommendations by prison administrators. The rules, adopted in 2015, found an overrepresentation of Indigenous peoples in federal correctional facilities; offenders are more likely to be incarcerated at a younger age, kept in custody longer, denied paroles, overrepresented in segregation, and assigned a high risk offender status. The United Nations Standard Minimum Rules for the Treatment of Prisoners have provided a leading international voice on the harms of solitary confinement for children, or any other punishment that may compromise the physical or mental health of juveniles.

The report also uncovered the prevalence of mental disorders in federal Canadian prisons remains significantly higher than in the community—about 2–4 times higher for psychosis and major depression, and ten times higher for antisocial personality disorder, with 70 per cent of men and 79 per cent of women having at least one DSM-N-TR diagnosis (see https://www.unodc.org/documents/justice-and-prison-reform/Nelson_Mandela_Rules-E-ebook.pdf, retrieved January 13, 2025).

Youth Culture and Incarceration

While there are many reasons why incarcerated youth may refuse support inside or outside of an institution, a significant contributing factor is undoubtedly the subculture of detained youth. In order to better understand the behavior, actions, and values of these youth, a common reference for the concepts of culture and subculture is necessary.

Citing Harris (1968), *culture* is defined as the practice and process of transmitting knowledge within and across generations. A more anthropological view is that culture is the 'meaning which people create, and which create people as members of societies' (p. 6)—and is in many ways, this is a "'collective' practice and process (Hannerz, 1992). Learned behavior, such as that found in institutions and groups, is thus, by definition, culture or cultural in some form. Following this, *subculture* can be understood as learned behavior in small groups, outside or alongside 'mainstream' society.

Fine and Kleinman (1991) further clarify or 'reconceptualize' the concept of subculture with the observation that subculture develops through 'an inter-locking group network characterized by multiple group membership, weak ties, structural roles ... [when the desire] to identify with the referent group serves to motivate the potential member to adopt ... the behaviors, norms and values characteristic of the subculture' (p. ii).

In theory, fostering positive mental, emotional, and physical development should be an integral part of the juvenile corrections process. Young people committing serious offences have captured headlines and media attention, from 'troubled' children to youth whom the public should fear, leading to policymakers lessening efforts to rehabilitate young offenders. Singer & McDowall (1988) state there is no empirical evidence that long sentences reduce youth crime.

Mary Stokrocki (2004) reports that contextual consideration, including the physical environment, social-cultural factors, and economic and political challenges are all important factors to consider with respect to art programs. She refers to art programs that take place in correctional facilities as 'marginalized settings.' Stokrocki cites Congdon (1984) who taught art in a Milwaukee county jail setting. Congdon concluded that the inclusion of inmates' interests, ideas, and concerns was paramount to successful teaching in such a restrictive context.

Note: Violent crimes committed by young women and girls receive significant media attention. Their actions are characterized as deviations from the gendered norms of society, especially given the reality that young women aged 15 to 18 account for 2.147 crimes per 100,000 versus the rate of 10,084 among young men in the same age group. These sexist biases also contribute to the higher rate of incarceration of young women as compared to men remanded or charged in similar circumstances.

Growing Up Behind Bars

T.S. writes of the oppressive life of 'corrections' and the many youth who spend the majority of their adolescent years in the justice system.

> *Prison*
>
> *These walls contain me, I am in a place that I hate, but I have learned to call it home. They call us criminals; I call us misguided. They see the evil, and I see the good. I try to help and explain to these people, but they block me out, 'cause in their eyes, I am not one of them. I am considered an outsider, and I will always be until my time comes. So for now, I sit here and watch and am the only one who knows the truth, because these people who consider themselves normal, are blinded by a wall. And this wall is called the youth justice system.*

American feminist, political activist, and philosopher Angela Davis maintains that prisons do not disappear problems, they disappear human beings. The primary objective of a correctional facility is security. Behavior modification techniques that serve to suppress individuality are used to achieve this aim. Behavior modification uses techniques to strengthen or weaken specific behaviors. Techniques that aim to weaken behaviors include 'time out', a procedure that removes the teen, sending them to their room. If the correctional officers feel their own security or the security of others on the unit is at risk, or the teen vocalizes threats of self-harm, the teen is brought to 'seg' (segregation)—a demeaning and degrading isolation room.

Confining young people, some under the age of 18, cuts them off from families and communities; disrupts their educations; and exposes them to further trauma and violence, affecting their overall development. In the U.S., imprisonment of children (17 and under) in adult correctional institutions is simply unconstitutional. A 2014 study of youth in Southern California who had recently been released from juvenile facilities found that 77 per cent reported suffering from one or more types of physical, sexual, or verbal abuse. The study also found that abuse *during* incarceration led to greater social and emotional problems following release, including post-traumatic stress reactions, depression symptoms, and continued criminal behavior (Dierkhising, Lane, & Natguaki, 2014).

Rettig (1980) agrees that detaining youth in an attempt to punish transgression ignores the warning that punished youth will often respond with continued deviance. He further explains that 'detained youth' sometimes begin to structure their identity around the label of 'delinquent'—the effect being future criminal behavior and diminished employment/educational opportunities.

In the following example of reflective writing, the writer reveals the youth subculture and its negative effects, and the psychological toll of being sentenced to years of confinement and 'doing time':

> *What does it mean to be in jail, what is it like to have no freedom? All I've ever known is to fail, thinking ... if I write poems will people ever read them? To me I'm dead, to others I'm dying, I've fucked my own life this I'm not denying, some days I want to die, some days I want to live, some days I want to take, and others I want to give. I can't completely explain my thoughts, because of all these blurry spots. This place will change your mind forever. It will leave your thoughts feeling blind and severed, some people say jail is easy like daycare, but the mental damage it will inflict forever will stay there. People can't just tell you what jail is like, because most will say it's easy ... like riding a bike. They will leave out what would really count. They would leave this out in large amounts. It's hard to say the damage it's done, but I'll tell you one thing it ain't no fun. All I want is to walk outside, but by jail rules I must abide. I now live my life for a second chance, most days I feel like I'm stuck in a trance. Some days I feel I could cry, there it goes dripping from the corner of my eye, but my time will come, where I can live once more, where I can go outside and have fun, or even walk to the store. People take advantage of freedom and how great it is, trust me I did it too but for my second chance I still live. Jail is cold and dark, not a pretty sight. I cannot find my spark, at the end of my tunnel there is no light, this is jail, in here no one will prevail.*
>
> (Anonymous)

Institutional subcultures, such as the one I observed in 'corrections', are known to have an especially strong impact on those exposed to them. The eminent French philosopher and sociologist Michel Foucault (1980) observed that the strongest subcultures exist in militaries, mental institutions, and prisons. The oft-quoted observation is consistent with my own experience with youth in custody—prison by any other name.

In some communities, juvenile detention facilities are simply the anticipated first stop on a road leading directly to the 'big league': adult prison. Confinement may not deter criminal behavior because the experience has become normalized—teens identify with an outlaw culture and can take on a 'gangster' persona. Speaking with teens who will be transferred from juvenile to adult facilities many say things such as, 'my father is in there, I'll be fine ...', thinking of it as a rite of passage.

The localized belief that going away to prison is normal is a direct consequence of certain groups being disproportionately incarcerated over the decades (Taylor, 2003). Being part of a young person's life is a privilege. Whether we barely touch the surface of their lives or become a life-altering mentor, our actions must be motivated by the very best intentions. We must always be respectful and remember that beneath these kids' tough exteriors, there may be goodness (Cruse, 2006, p. 65).

The reality is that many young people make choices regarding drug use, criminal behavior, violence, prostitution, and street life because their options are limited. Upon release from a correctional institution, youth all too often return to the same conditions that precipitated their criminal activities in the first place. American scholar of juvenile delinquency Albert K. Cohen advocated for better resources and understanding of the special needs and dilemmas faced by young people reintegrating into society: '[T]heir homes, if they had one, were not places where they could feel self-assured and safe, but areas where they came to feel worse about themselves, emotionally alienated and confirmed their sense of themselves as flawed, unworthy young people ... then they begin to see themselves as outsiders' (cited in Currie, 2004, p. 50)

Upon release, not all adolescents return to their communities and/or families. Youth had often mentioned of their concerns (and reality) of reintegrating into society—of overcrowded group homes, and placements where they did not feel welcome. They often expressed feeling they were only there for the money supplement the foster parent(s) received from the government, and it was heart-breaking to hear them express feelings of neglect.

> *They wanted me out of the house while their family spent Christmas holidays...told me I could only take a shower for a brief time 'cause of lack of hot water ... there was no food and when I asked for a peanut butter sandwich, he told me to wait until he finished watching his program on TV ...*

An investigative report by Public Works & Government Services stated:

> Corrections Services Canada continues not to recognize the need to provide special housing, programming or other services for younger prisoners. While privately most acknowledge that they are ill-equipped to meet the needs of young prisoners, and so they are mostly kept isolated, the official position is that programs available to all prisoners can be adapted to meet the needs of younger prisoners.
>
> (Sapers, 2005–2006, p. 17)

PTSD and Rehabilitation

Rehabilitation means to restore to a normal life after a period of illness or imprisonment. The assumption of rehabilitation is that rather than punishing an individual, rehabilitation would seek, by means of education or therapy, to bring him or her into an attitude that would be helpful, rather than harmful to society (see https://en.wikipedia.org/wiki/Rehabilitation_(penology), retrieved January 2, 2020). This includes maintaining ties to the outside world and learning new skills to assist them with working life on the outside.

Research shows traumatic stress changes the structure of the brain, hard-wiring it to protect against danger. This can cause youth to live in 'survival mode' making it extremely hard for them to develop positive coping mechanisms—incarceration is not the solution. Although many adults and young offenders refer to youth custody centers as 'juvie', despite the attempt to soften the label of a correctional facility, it still remains a difficult 'rite of passage' for many young people.

Life 'inside' begins when a teen enters the admissions area in handcuffs and leg shackles. Within an hour, the young male or female is stripped of all personal effects such as clothing, money, phones, etc., and strip-searched for contraband. After a mandatory shower, they are given the center's clothing and escorted to their cell. Whether one is employed as line staff (correctional officers) or as program staff (teachers, counselors, and administrators), a correctional facility is a repressive workplace. There are strictly enforced daily regiments and there is a constant risk for both staff and teens in regards to personal safety or witnessing violent behaviors, whether physical or verbal.

I draw the reader's attention to the 'Purpose of Youth Sentence', outlined in the Youth Criminal Justice Act (YCJA), 'to hold the youth accountable for the offense by imposing sanctions that have meaningful consequences for the youth and that *promote their rehabilitation and reintegration* into society [italics mine] thereby contributing to the long term protection of society' (internal document/Youth sentences/Summary/Purpose, 2006, p. 19).

Recommendations in the YCJA include:

- Every reasonable opportunity will be given to parents, extended family and the community to be involved with and assist in responding to the needs of youth.
- Preventing re-offending is more effectively achieved when youth are required to assume and exercise responsibility for the control of their own behavior.
- The resolution of youth's conflict with the law is, wherever feasible, most appropriately afforded through the opportunity to make amends and through the use of community-based programs.
- Optimal opportunities for continued interactions with the community will be afforded to youth whenever the removal of the youth from the community occurs and, while in a place of confinement, access to opportunities and resources normally available in the community should, to the greatest extent feasible, be made available.

Institutions (of any kind) reward those who follow the rules and support the status quo. There is often little room anywhere in society for adolescents to find a constructive outlet for self-expression and the questioning of authority. This is especially true for teens subjected to that most rigid of institutions—the correctional institution. Working with youth who have engaged in or are witnesses of serious violence is challenging: they often struggle with low self-esteem due to histories of family instability, conflict, and abuse. Vulnerable to exploitation, they are often distrustful of any 'system' imposed on them. Thus, I believe it is extremely important to build mutual trust and respect while creating a safe, non-judgmental environment where they can express themselves and be recognized and *valued* as individuals, having their needs understood and met.

What 'institutional systems' can take away is a sense of identity and confidence in human interaction. Juvenile detention centers provide little in the way of coping skills when youth are released—it is difficult to address self-esteem, education, and occupational training when individuals are lacking the basics while detained: safe living conditions, quality educational instruction, and high-quality mental and physical health services.

Upon release, many will face a return to unsafe homes, shelter placements akin to adult foster care, and the receipt of a new label—one of society's 'undesirables'. In the following example of reflective writing, a teen shares with readers:

> *Shed Tears*
>
> *How can I finish life, if I don't know how to start? How can I keep living with a cold heart? How is this blood still flowing through my veins? And how do I keep ending up in these chains? Why can't I change my criminal ways? It's not like I enjoy spending jail days. Once you're in the system, it's hard to get out, because society fills your head with nothing but doubt. I need my family and my family needs me. And I'm sitting in prison when I could be free. Is this my last sentence, am I really done? Or will I get out and just start to run. No, this is it I'm done wasting my time. I don't need to live a life of crime. I have wasted well over seven years. And all I have to show are these shed tears.*
>
> (Anonymous)

Youth Development Theory and Incarceration

Youth development professionals see *potential* and not *pathology* when looking at the youth they serve (McLaughlin, 2000). Development is viewed as occurring on many levels simultaneously: biological, psychological, interpersonal, familial, societal, cultural, physical, ecological, and historical (Ford & Lerner, 1992).

Developmental theory is largely based on studies of white, middle-class, male, non-incarcerated youth. If developmental theory is to become relevant to the experiences of a broad range of adolescents, researchers must address how high rates of youth violence, arrests, and incarceration *affect* development. Absent information on disadvantaged youth must reflect on those developmental issues that are thought to apply to all adolescents. The lack of research in this area is especially problematic for BIPOC male and female youths who can experience the greatest likelihood of being justice-involved.

Rettig, in his 1980 article, 'Considering the use and usefulness of juvenile detention: Operationalizing social theory,' found that many practitioners resort to detention as a matter of convenience rather than as an attempt to meet the needs of the youth involved. Programs that incorporate best practice principles of youth development will increase their overall wellbeing and enhance youth development theory, as compared to what occurs among those who are confined in typical detention settings.

In the case of using the arts for purposes of reconciliation and rehabilitation, a distinction has to be made between using art as an end in itself, and using art as a means to achieve an additional goal. An example of the latter would be an emphasis on the need for prison art programs with merit-based incentives such as community engagement and early release.

Substance Use Disorder and Street Life

Research has demonstrated that substance abuse is a key need area for young offenders and can contribute to their criminal activity. In order for substance abuse treatment to be effective, it should target multiple areas: family, academic, employment, as well as other personal factors experienced upon release from a correctional facility with relapse prevention strategies. The following is an excerpt by an anonymous teen on addiction:

> *You try to live in a normal society, but you've been rejected. You resort to prostitution as a solution. Life for you is just an illusion. You're considered a whore, and the pimp you work for says you're no good anymore. You soon decide your only option is suicide, but no one cares or cries because it's just another junkie who died. Little do they realize you were once a beautiful baby. They can't hear you screaming, 'save me'. Someone who was once a person's miracle has now become someone who's hysterical. It brings nothing but pain to know, troubled youths having nothing but drugs to gain.*

In the following excerpt of 'Misery', T. shares gang life on the streets:

> *Life as a G,... I blend among the frozen hearted. Grew up with roaches all around like my bro's apartment. Earth is hell and we just waiting for the flames to rise. Gas is hopeless fire when angels cry. I wear a smile trying to cover up the pain inside. Fighting to live but truth is I can't wait to die. As a troubled youth, fascinated by money and drugs, I saw my childhood say goodbye. Loving the streets with all my heart got me into no things.*

An anonymous contributor addresses 'drug addiction' through the lens of 'change'. He examines a recurring theme shared by other young writers that surfaced in many issues of *Inside-Out Magazine*, our prison publication—teens can successfully reintegrate with social supports from a variety of people in the community, yet too often these supports either don't exist or are not in place prior to their release. With positive peer mentors to identify with, and programming that focuses on helping them develop and see their *strengths* instead of their mistakes, adolescents can begin to consider a better future.

> *Hope ... on Life's Terms*
> *What is this thing we call 'drug addiction'?*
> *Our lives revolve around it, but still there is no cure.*
> *Deprivation, death, sorrow, these are the things we get out of it,*
> *And yet it feels like home.*
> *Our minds are corrupted by this substance; man-made, and we feel invincible.*
> *Loneliness, and unloved is what we know.*
> *Hate and violence is what we do, but things can change.*
> *The next feelings might be of hope and courage.*
> *And yet this all gets washed away by out next hit.*
> *Why do we do this to ourselves? Why did I do this to myself?*
> *I've seen death, felt deprivation, and witnessed sorrow, but I'm hooked.*
> *Life seems worthless; but yet once again I feel hope.*
> *This hope gets me through the day, and hopefully tomorrow.*
> *So for anyone who has this disease of addition, just remember, that even though you seem at the bottom, it's only a few steps further to the top!*

There is also a large pool of children who are not clinically ill but who need more adult support to help them develop the emotional resiliency, coping skills, and academic successes that will help prevent risks such as substance abuse, gang involvement, teen pregnancy, and school drop-out (Noam & Hermann, 2002). Their stories are being told for a reason and we need to listen.

Intersection between Mental Health and the Juvenile Justice System

Mental disorders relate to issues or difficulties a person may experience with his or her psychological, emotional, and social wellbeing. Certain risk factors could increase the occurrence of both mental health and problem behaviors in youths. For example, exposure to violence can increase mental health issues, such as post-traumatic stress, and increase the occurrence of delinquent behavior (Finkelhor et al., 2009).

Among maltreated youths living in out-of-home care, the presence of a mental health disorder was significantly associated with juvenile justice system involvement, and conduct disorder was the strongest predictor (Yampolskaya and Chuang, 2012) (for additional research, see: Richard Mendel, Senior Research Fellow for Youth Justice, Advocacy for Reform, http://sentencingproject.org, retrieved January 13, 2025).

Trauma and exposure to violence may also increase the likelihood of juvenile justice involvement. Multiple studies show a connection between childhood violence exposure and antisocial behavior, including delinquency, gang involvement, substance use, post-traumatic stress disorder, anxiety, depression, and aggression (Wilson, Stover, and Berkowitz, 2009; Finkelhor et al., 2009). We must listen to matters that concern them and attempt to replace the punitive and retributive nature of orthodox justice with a model of restoration and healing based on the future and not the transgressions of the past (Schissel, 1997).

Young people need support to develop a healthy self-identity; without that, healthy coping habits are near impossible to achieve, and without mentorship and support, it is easy to give up. They also need a social network that supports and provides them with opportunities to interact and learn from each other, from adult mentors, and from community members. It is imperative that we provide these youth with powerful new methods of responding to the challenges they face in the present so they can build a foundation for healthy, productive, and fulfilling lives in the future.

Multiple interventions are required to meet the needs of youth in custody in order for them to reintegrate successfully into the community. Youth development professionals see *potential* and not *pathology* when looking at the youth they serve (McLaughlin, 2000). Participation is health-enhancing in and of itself, a way of empowering young people and recognizing their capabilities, and establishes adolescents and adults as *partners* providing a foundation based on the strengths and competencies of working together. Further, this action acknowledges the 'authority of experience' of the teenager and the validity of experiential learning as part of a positive concept of mental health (Denshire, 1994).

Every generation faces the challenge of preserving, and hopefully, improving the quality of life in our communities. Through social inclusion and community engagement, critical thinking, peer support and leadership training, young people can develop the skills they need to meet this complex challenge. We accomplish this by building mutual trust and respect while creating a safe, non-judgmental environment where justice-involved youth can express themselves, and be recognized and valued as individuals having their needs understood and met.

In this excerpt of 'Reality on the Inside', C. shares his views on how youth with personal histories characterized by neglect and lack of supervision/parental involvement, can easily get caught in the web of street life and addiction. His 'rap' lyrics were highly regarded by many in and out of corrections—because many had firsthand knowledge of the topics he addressed.

> *Locked up in a room where they keep you away from your life like a pause, a consequence, a rock bottom experience. Put you in a place where the trees laugh at you, the walls breath heavy and your brain runs faster than a flash. 'What ifs' are going through your head, and as the walls breathe louder and louder your dreams become more real … now I have to face my consequences. This took more than my summer away—took time away from friends, moments with family, and Kodak pictures with my girl. And I look back and think—was it worth it …? You're locked away; not gone.*

For those youths moving out of the justice system, readjusting back into society can be very difficult. They need resources to help them make decisions that will enable them to resolve their problems and survive; they require information and support to make good choices for education and work, and to rebuild relationships with their communities, family, and friends. Engaging them in positive youth development activities, and addressing any needs or problems that might be interfering with their success and wellbeing, will provide the foundation they need. We also need to step back from countless reports and statistics and see the causes of delinquency as '*socially produced*' [italics mine] and work on programs that really are in 'the best interests' of young people (O'Bireck, 1996, p. 191).

Participation is health-enhancing in and of itself, a way of empowering young people and recognizing their capabilities. Youth participation establishes adolescents and adults as *partners* and provides a foundation based on strengths and competence of working together. Further, this action acknowledges the 'authority of experience' of the teenager and the validity of experiential learning as part of a positive concept of mental health. It is also a means of *changing* the mental health system to make it more responsive to young people (Denshire, 1994).

The following is an example of a youth-driven project for and with incarcerated teens. This research project qualified as minimal risk as the youth were not at risk of emotional harm since I was not asking them to re-visit the issues that brought them into custody. On the contrary, I was engaging them in a productive and pro-social learning activity. Art and education projects can play an important role in engaging young people, and in the case of this project, they reconnected (albeit on the 'inside') with their home communities—and resources that were *sanctioned* (or not) by them. This project embraced not only their creative needs, but also provided them with a real sense of accomplishment and a *positive learning experience*.

The Resource Guide

In *The Outside Guide* research project, participants combined their skills to work on a self-directed project they knew from personal experience would be of benefit to their peers. They took on various technical and production roles, learned new computer design skills, and mastered design software programs. They also learned to gather information and present their findings to their peers at weekly meetings. They took ownership—although each individual had to be able to hold up his or her own responsibilities, each did so with a view of connection and a link to the finished project. Youth had to make decisions on the overall content of the publication—what went in and what didn't. Additionally, they recognized the interdependence of their peers, their individual roles in the project, and the coordination needed when working within the confines of a correctional institution (reviewed in Chapter 5, 'The Projects').

Conclusion

'Rehabilitation' is more effective when individuals have a stake in the process, and development theorists tend to overlook the potentially vital role that community organizations can play in improving lives, particularly for those who are marginalized in society and do not have a legitimate voice. Post-treatment factors represent those areas that can be targeted by criminal justice agencies for the provision of aftercare services, thus identifying and enhancing protective factors. Few studies have explored the effectiveness of these services.

Institutional subcultures, such as the one I observed as a youth counselor, are known to have an especially strong impact on those exposed to them. The eminent French philosopher and sociologist Michel Foucault (1980) observed that the strongest subcultures exist in militaries, mental institutions, and prisons. This oft-quoted observation is consistent with my own experience with a custody center —prison by any other name. In the public discussion of youth problems, specifically justice-involved teens, the least heard voices are often those most deeply affected. Chapter 5 introduces youth-driven projects at the correctional facility and the positive factors that programs provide to those young people grasping for identity in a rigid structure not of their own making.

Chapter 3 draws attention to community organizations in supporting justice-involved youth. In it, I introduce the concept of 'community justice' and the psychosocial development of children and adolescents, their overall health and emotional wellbeing, and then continue the discussion of creating educational experiences that empower young people whilst demonstrating the positive difference community programs can have on their lives.

References

Bertram, C. (2010). Fetal Alcohol Spectrum Disorder: Motor-skill activities hold promise of rewiring children's damaged brains. *The Globe and Mail.*

Cruse, J. (2006). *Juvie: Inside Canada's youth jails.* Vancouver: Granville Island.

Currie, E. (2004). *The Road to Whatever.* New York: Henry Holt.

Delgado, M. (2006). *New Frontiers for Youth Development in the Twenty-First Century: Revitalizing and broadening youth development.* New York: Columbus University Press.

Denshire, S. (1994). *The Shape and Impact of Youth Participation in Health.* Working paper prepared for Study Group on Young People and Health for all by the Year 2000. Geneva, Switzerland: World Health Organization.

Dierkhising, C.B., Lane, A., & Natguaki, M.N. (2014). Victims behind bars: A preliminary study of abuse during juvenile incarceration and post-release social and emotional functions. *Psychology, Public Policy & Law*, 20(2), 181.

Evan-Egar, E. (2017). *The Choice: Embrace the possible.* New York: Scribner.

Fine, G.A. & Kleinman, S. (1991). *Rethinking Subculture: An interactionist analysis.* St. Paul, MN: University of Minnesota.

Finkelhor, D., Turner, H., Ormrod, R., Hamby, S., & Kracke, K. (2009). Children's exposure to violence: A comprehensive national survey. *Juvenile Justice Bulletin.* Washington, DC: U.S. Department of Justice, Office of Justice Programs, Office of Juvenile Justice and Delinquency Prevention.

Ford, J.D., Chapman, J.F., Hawke, J., & Albert, D. (2007). *Trauma among Youth in the Juvenile Justice System: Critical issues and new directions.* Delmar, N.Y.: National Center for Mental Health and Juvenile Justice.

Ford, D.H., & Lerner, R.M. (1992). *Developmental Systems Theory: An integrative approach*. Thousand Oaks, CA: Sage Inc.
Foucault, M. (1980). *Power/Knowledge: Selected interviews and other writings, 1972–1977*. New York: Pantheon.
Hannerz, U. (1992). *Cultural Complexity: Studies in the social organization of meaning*. Columbia, OH: Columbia University Press.
Harris, M. (1968). *The Rise of Anthropological Theory: A history of theories of culture*. Calgary, AB: Mira Press.
Klonsky, E.D., Victor, S.E., & Saffer, B.Y. (2014). Non-suicidal Self-injury: What we know and what we need to know. *Canadian Journal of Psychiatry*, 59(11), 565–568.
Kools, S.M. (1997). Adolescent identity development in foster care. *Family Relations*, 46(3), 263–271.
Kurtz, Z.R., Thornes, R., & Bailey, S. (1998). Children in the criminal justice and secure care systems. How their mental health needs are met. *Journal of Adolescence*, 21(5), 543–553.
McCreary Centre Society (2002). Youth participation: What is it about? Retrieved September 27, 2008 from www.mes.bc.ca/ya_base.htm.
McLaughlin, M. (2000). *Community Counts: How youth organizations matter for youth development*. Washington, DC: Public Education Network. Retrieved September 25, 2009 from www.publiceducation.org/cgi/bin/download-manager/publication/p.72.asp.
Menzies, P. (2008). Developing an Aboriginal healing model for intergenerational trauma. *International Journal of Health Promotion and Education*, 46(2), 17.
Noam, G.G., & Hermann, C.A. (2002). Where education and mental health meet: Developmental prevention and early intervention in schools. *Development and Psychopathology*, 14, 861–875.
O'Bireck, G.M. (Ed.) (1996). *Not a Kid Anymore: Canadian youth, crime, and subcultures*. Scarborough, ON: Thomson Canada.
Rettig, R.P. (1980). Considering the use and usefulness of juvenile detention: Operationalizing social theory. *Adolescence*, 58(15), 443–459.
Sapers, H. (2005–2006). *Annual Report of the Correctional Investigator*. Ottawa: Minister of Public Works & Government Services Canada.
Schissel, B. (1997). *Blaming Children: Youth crime, moral panics and the politics of hate*. Black Press: Fernwood Publishing.
Siegesmund, R. (1998). Why do we teach art today? *Studies in Art Education*, 39(3), 197–215.
Silverstein, S. (1973). The adolescent waiting room. *Social Work*, 18(6), 105–107.
Singer, S. & McDowall, D. (1988). Criminalizing delinquency: The deterrent effects of the New York Juvenile Offender Law. *Law and Society Review*, 23(3), 521–535.
Solomon, A. (2022). The mystifying rise of child suicide: A family tragedy sheds light on a burgeoning mental-health emergency. *The New Yorker*, April 4, 2022.
Stokrocki, M. (2004). *Contexts for teaching art*. In E. Eisner & M. Day (Eds.) (pp. 439–466). Mahwah, NJ: Lawrence Erlbaum.
Taylor, K. (2003). *Growing up Behind Bars: Confinement, youth development, and crime*. East Lansing, MI: Michigan State University.
Waldram, J. (1994). Aboriginal spirituality in corrections: A Canadian case study in religion and therapy. *American Indian Quarterly*, 18(2), 197–214.
Wilcock, A.A. (1998). *An Occupational Perspective on Health*. Thorofare, NJ: Slack.
Wilson, H.W., Stover, C.S., & Berkowitz, S.J. (2009). Research review: The relationship between childhood violence and exposure and juvenile antisocial behavior: A meta-analytic review. *Journal of Childhood Psychology and Psychiatry*, 50(7), 769–779.
Wilson, S. (2000). *Fragments: A narrative approach to arts-based research* (unpublished thesis). University of British Columbia, BC.
Yampolskaya, S. & Chuang, E. (2012). Effects of mental health disorders on the risk of juvenile justice system involvement and recidivism among children placed in out-of-home care. *American Journal of Orthopsychiatry*, 82(4), 585–593.

Chapter 3

Community Regeneration

Making the Connection

Introduction

This chapter discusses the concept of 'community justice' and the psychosocial development of children and adolescents, as well as their overall health and emotional wellbeing. It then continues the discussion of creating educational experiences that empower young people and the positive difference community programs can have on their lives.

Youth development theorists tend to *overlook* the potentially vital role that community organizations can play in improving the lives of youth, particularly those who are 'marginalized' in society and without a legitimate voice. These young people especially need help to shape their identities and determine their destinies.

Cognitive development, creative growth, and emotional learning are linked. What 'institutional systems' can take away is a sense of identity and confidence in human interactions, especially in the case of former detained youth who upon release can begin to structure their identity around the label 'delinquent'; the effect being future criminal behavior, diminished employment and educational opportunities, and the receipt of a new label—one of society's 'undesirables'.

> Zero tolerance means none or nothing. Tolerance gestures toward an understanding, generosity, kindness, benevolence, justice, and forgiveness. We need to teach and practice tolerance. Exerting 'power over' children fuels the jail industrial complex but does nothing to advance our collective aspirations.
>
> (Jackson Sr., 2000, foreword)

Community Justice

Community justice is a fairly recent development with a mission to help community residents manage their own affairs, solve their own problems, and live together effectively and safely.

'Goals are best achieved by giving everyone a stake in the quality of community life. To achieve this mission, community justice involves risk assessment and control of offenders, victim restoration, community contracting, and cost sharing' (Clear & Karp, 1998, p. 55). I refer to the Youth Criminal Justice Act in Chapter 2, which represented a new strategy toward the administration of youth justice in Canada. The Act was intended to promote accountability and responsibility while encouraging *alternatives* to imprisonment through the use of community-based sentences, with a focus on rehabilitation, reintegration, and

DOI: 10.4324/9781003534082-3

reparation. This approach is intended to 'provide immediate and long-term responses to youth crime by building links to *community-based* youth crime prevention programs and to initiatives that address the root causes of criminal behaviors' (Department of Justice, Serving Canadians, Youth Justice Research, 2003, internal document).

'Giving responsibility and expecting accountability is at the core of most successful community initiatives ... people are learning by doing, and the community's experiencing positive ripple effects' (Richmond, 2000). According to Garland (2001), adults responsible for their care 'forget that youth have a lot of anger and outrage to be dealt with and not medicated. They need to deal with their issues through discussion and dialogue, and not dulled out and numbed with drugs' (p. 46). Instead of communicating how badly they feel, teens may act out and be irritable toward others. Such behaviors are commonly misinterpreted and are frequently labeled 'disobedient and out of control.' The public may believe that denial of rights of individuals in custody is justified by the fact that they have presented themselves as unwilling or unable to conduct themselves in society, though Garland asserts this argument has *no* merit.

Incarceration versus Community

> Each and every day across America, we are leaving children behind. In our state legislature, on our school boards, in our schools, and in our homes, we have given up on American's great promise—our children. When we commit to leaving no child behind, we are motivated to nurture rather than punish, to intervene rather than incarcerate, and to love rather than loathe. Children conform to the dictates and expectations of their environment. If we desire loving children, we must create loving environments.
>
> (Jackson Sr., 2000, foreword)

Creative activities are a rich way to express inner thoughts and feelings. Confinement hinders the process of development by *disrupting* young people's opportunities to learn, grow, and participate in essential rites of passage associated with adolescent development. Incarceration is a failed strategy for rehabilitating youth and ignores adolescent development research (see Mendel, 2023).

Emotional Development

Daniel Goleman (cited in Gardner, 1999) states that we should not negate the importance of one's own emotional life. The term 'emotional intelligence' was popularized in 1995 by professors of psychology and researchers Peter Salovey and John Mayer, and suggests a spectrum of emotional abilities, including an ability to understand one's own and others' emotions to promote listening and empathetic skills. The world would be more hospitable, Goleman states, if we cultivated emotional intelligence as diligently as we now promote cognitive intelligence. Unfortunately, working toward a more smoothly functioning family or community is not generally considered within the realm of intelligence.

Gardner (1999) also affirms the need for an education that takes into consideration existential intelligence, or a concern with 'ultimate' issues, and provides an example of individuals who undergo tremendous pain—whether physical, psychic, or both—feeling estranged from their habitual world. Although I recognize Gardner is referring to physical pain and physiological issues, I would like to expand on this to include those who have suffered psychological and emotional violence, resulting in post-traumatic stress disorder (PTSD). They need guidance to channel their symptoms and pain. I have observed adolescents in my programs exhibit a high level of insight. Perhaps this is because they have found a community of like-minded individuals where they feel comfortable sharing their views and beliefs. This reaffirms my belief in community programs for those who don't, or can't, 'make it' in a mainstream educational setting.

Reverend Jesse L. Jackson Sr. (2000) believes that when legislators and school administrators recognize that all children have potential, they legislate differently and channel resources toward educating and away from incarcerating.

Art as Education and Therapy

I have always found the creative arts to be beneficial for young people moving towards healing and growth, providing an outlet for self-expression and a means of building self-esteem. Advocacy statements and studies by various arts education associations provide strong support for this. Some of these influential organizations include the National Campaign for the Arts (U.K.), Americans for the Arts (U.S.A.), the National Art Education Association (U.S.A.), and the Canadian Society for Education through Art. The supporting arguments from these and many other groups are familiar to readers of art education material, especially in supporting K-12 education. Unfortunately, as one Brooklyn teacher put it, the present emphasis suggest that 'We care more about how well school children can read and write than whether they'll be alive next week' (cited in Goleman, 1995, p. 231).

The 'Business' of Incarceration

Davis (2003) states that the prison system relieves us of the responsibility of seriously engaging with the 'problems of our society':

> The prison ... functions ideologically as an abstract site in which undesirables are deposited, relieving us of the responsibility of thinking about the real issues afflicting those communities from which prisoners are drawn in such disproportionate numbers ...
>
> (p. 8)

Community interventions cost a small fraction of the price of incarceration. In Canada, the current cost is approximately $259.00 daily per youth, and $318.00 daily per adult (Public Safety Canada, 2022). On average, one year of confinement has been estimated to cost an average of $214,000.00, and is operated by federal and provincial governments. The only private adult prison in Canada was the maximum-security Central North Correctional Centre in Penetanguishene, Ontario, Canada, operated by the U.S.-based Management and Trainings Corporation from its opening in 2001 through to the end of its first contract period in 2006 (Correctional Services Canada, viewed on https://www.canada.ca in August 2024).

As of 2018, 40 per cent of residential detention facilities in the United States were private, housing 27 per cent of imprisoned youth, according to the U.S. Office of Juvenile Justice and Delinquency Prevention, U.S. Department of Justice. A total of 27 states and the federal government use private corporations to run some of their correctional facilities. Each year, non-profit and for-profit detention centers rake in millions of taxpayer dollars. Florida has more than $800 million in multiyear contracts with private providers. Audits, lawsuits, and accusations from youth and former staff members point to inconsistent oversight, as well a physical and sexual abuse by staff and other youth. (http://kidsimprisoned.new21.com/, retrieved June 24, 2024).

Social Intelligence and Collaboration

In a custodial setting, helping teens resolve conflicts and disagreements peacefully can aid in socializing and group situations. Simply put, it is through how we interact with others in social situations particularly 'in turbulent social currents' that social intelligence can help the adolescent transform a potentially hostile situation into a positive outcome. Collaborative art programs can develop social intelligence—teens socialize with peers and learn not to compete with one another, but instead to collaborate in order to obtain shared results. Most importantly, collaborating on projects with incarcerated teens offers a positive experience to help them regain what institutional systems and the circumstances of their lives sometimes obliterate—a sense of individual identity and confidence in human interaction.

In the case of painting a mural, for example, they collaborated on the initial design, decided on colors, and painted the image. In the spirit of cooperation, they worked together toward a common goal—to improve their dismal surroundings. Their artistic efforts became a source of pride for the teens who painted and even for those who assisted with minor tasks like cleaning paintbrushes, pans, and water containers or merely watched as the work was created. The final image would be photographed to appear on the cover of an issue of *Inside-Out Magazine*.

Culturally Responsive Programs

The annual incarceration rate (2018–2019) of Canadian Aboriginal youth was 64.5 per 10,000 population compared to 8.2 per 10,000 for non-Aboriginal youth (in other words, they are eight times more likely to be in custody compared to their non-Aboriginal counterparts.) While inside, efforts should be made for youths to connect to community programs that will be specific to their needs upon release.

Encouraging literacy, self-expression, some critical thinking skills, and healthy supportive relationships with adults and their community, *The Beat Within*, a publication of writing and art from the inside, partners with community organizations and individuals to bring resources to youth *both* inside and outside detention; to provide a bridge between youths who are locked up and the community that aims to support their progress towards healthy, non-violent, and productive lives.

Implementing expressive art programs in correctional facilities for inmates coming from other countries of origin can shine light on discriminatory or uneven treatment leading to difficult but vital social conversations. These programs can be both organized and informal, but we should never assume authority over people and issues we have had no firsthand experience with.

Social Inclusion and Mental Health

Positive social support is associated with improved mental health. Accessible and consistent community programs increase social reintegration, providing an alternative space to construct positive relationships that may be missing in lives. In addition to stress-reducing therapeutic benefits, they provide a vehicle and the safe space to openly express feelings, both positive and painful, and this is a common and effective way of coping with powerful emotions. When the program participants I worked with were given the opportunity to represent their experiences through various art forms, they often revealed insights that I believe they would have found difficult to articulate outside the environment of the program.

Conclusion

My counseling philosophy is based on a belief in the individual's innate strengths, capabilities, and the desire for wellness, and I acknowledge that not every one of us is comfortable with traditional 'talk therapy'. Providing alternate modes of personal expression is instrumental in promoting mental health and wellbeing. Especially for those teens that are 'confined', art can promote mental health by providing a safe environment to relieve stresses of separation from families, loss of freedom and choice, and the many other stress-inducing factors of incarceration.

Collaboration between mental health practitioners, policymakers, and various other health professionals provides an additional prevention education for system-involved youth to better prepare them for transitioning to society. Clear and Rose (2006) argue that an over-reliance on incarceration as a formal control can hinder the ability and weaken family and community structures. They add that at the ecological level, the side effects of policies intended to fight crime by controlling individual behavior may only exacerbate the problems they are intended to address.

References

Clear, T.R., & Karp, D.R. (1998). *Community Justice: An emerging field* (see page 55). Lanham, Maryland: Rowman & Littlefield.

Clear, T.R. & Rose, D.R. (2006). Incarceration, social capital, and crime: Implications for social disorganization theory *Criminology*, 36(3),441–480

Cross, C. (2018/2019). *Juvenile Justice and Expressive Arts: Creative disruptions through art programs for and with teens in a correctional institution*. London and New York: Routledge (Innovations in Corrections series).

Cruse, G. (2006). *Juvie: Inside Canada's youth jails*. Vancouver: Granville Island.

Davis, A.Y. (2003). *Are Prisons Obsolete?* New York: Seven Stories Press.

Ford, J.D., Chapman, J.F., Hawke, J., & Albert, D. (2007). *Trauma among Youth in the Juvenile Justice System: Critical issues and new directions*. Delmar, N.Y.: National Center for Mental Health and Juvenile Justice.

Gardner, H. (1999). *Intelligence Reframed: Multiple intelligences for the 21st century*. New York: Basic Books.

Garland, D. (2001). *The Culture of Control: Crime and social order in contemporary society*. Oxford: Oxford University Press.

Goleman, D. (1995). *Emotional intelligence: Why it can matter more than IQ*. New York: Bantam Books.

Goleman, D. (2006). *Social Intelligence: The new science of human relationships*. New York: Random House.

Jackson Sr., J.L. (2000). Foreword. In W. Ayers, R. Ayers, & B. Dohrn (Eds.) *Resisting Zero Tolerance*. New York: The New Press.

Mendel, R.A. (2023) Why youth incarceration fails: An updated review of the evidence. Retrieved December 22, 2024 from http://sentencing project.org/reports/why-youth-incarceration-fails-an updated-review-of-the-evidence.

Public Safety Canada (2022). Retrieved December 22, 2024 from publicsafety.qc.ca/cnt/srcs/pubctns/2017-h05-cp/index-en.aspx.

Richmond, J. (2000). New partnerships and new systems: Supporting young people's growth and job readiness. *CYD Journal*, 1, 20–25.

Sapers, H. (2005-2006). *Annual Report of the Correctional Investigator*. Ottawa: Minister of Public Works & Government Services Canada.

Chapter 4

Community as a Place to Begin

Introduction

This chapter discusses community programs and centers as an alternative environment to construct positive relationships that may be missing in youths' lives in addition to their role in providing stress-reducing therapeutic benefits, and my experience setting up a non-profit after-school violence intervention program for youth 'at risk'.

Young people aren't born young offenders. Community programs provide an alternative environment to construct positive relationships that may be missing in youths' lives, in addition to stress-reducing therapeutic benefits. They provide a vehicle for participants to openly express their feelings, both positive and painful, which is a common and effective way for coping with emotions. When program participants that I have worked with were given the opportunity to represent their experiences through various art forms, they often revealed insights that, at times, many would have found difficulty to articulate.

Eisner (1999) defines community as 'where open dialogue occurs between (and among) members and leaders, not where one group dominates or constantly pushes its own interests to the forefront...those who know precisely what other people should be doing often leave no space for diversity or for debate' (pp. 188–191).

Social Justice and Community

> 'Without community, there is no liberation ... but community must not mean a shedding of our differences, nor the pathetic pretense that these differences do not exist'
>
> (Lorde, 1995).

Every generation faces the challenge of preserving, and hopefully improving, the quality of life in our communities. The creative arts can do this by encouraging communication about personal identity and social issues through exposure to workshops in visual and media arts, creative writing, and critical thinking, developing the skills needed to meet this complex challenge. I believe adolescents want and should have a voice in shaping their communities and their world. This is not to say that youth don't speak but they are restricted from speaking in those spheres where public conversation shapes social policy (Giroux, 2003). Programs can take place in a variety of spaces including community centers, schools, juvenile halls, prisons, group homes, and recovery centers.

DOI: 10.4324/9781003534082-4

Social Engagement

Institutions (of any kind) reward those who follow the rules and support the status quo. There is often little room anywhere in society for adolescents to find a constructive outlet for self-expression and the questioning of authority. Giroux (2003) notes that when youth do speak, their voices generally emerge on the margins of society—in underground magazines, alternative music spheres, online blogs, and other subcultural sites. He argues that although relations between youth and adults have always been marked by strained generational and ideological struggles, today's youth also face '... a callous indifference to their spiritual and material needs ... one that indicates that the young have become our lowest national priority' (p. 2). I concur with Giroux (2003) that art, education, and cultural work have the ability to reinvent spaces for ethical and pedagogical practices, to create alliances, and produce social practices and policies that rewrite the importance of what it means to treat our youth with dignity. This is especially true for teens subjected to that most rigid of institutions—the correctional institution. Working with youth who have engaged in or are witnesses of serious violence is challenging; they often struggle with low self-esteem due to histories of family instability, conflict, and abuse. Social-based problems require *social* programs, not control programs.

Writing on the potential of art programs in correctional facilities, art educator Phyllis Kornfeld claims that they aid in emotional wellbeing of American adult inmates. Kornfeld (1997) has described the creation of art within the penitentiary art studio as being 'one of the few defences an inmate has against the dehumanizing effects of incarceration' (p. 7). I agree with Congdon (1984) who taught an art program in a Milwaukee county jail setting, that the inclusion of inmates' interests, ideas, and concerns is paramount to successful teaching in such a restrictive environment. Supplies are a major concern in correctional facilities.

Creativity and Alternative Learning Centers

Creative art workshops can provide both engaging and invigorating ways of learning that capture the attention and appeal to the many kinds of experiences that make today's youth who they are, and are adaptable to a variety of spaces including community centers, after-school programs, juvenile halls, prisons, group homes, and recovery centers. For juvenile offenders on probation, how well the class performs is often the result of whether or not the students are in the class on a voluntary or involuntary basis—authority figures summon an adversarial dynamic for students.

Not all alternative learning centers (ALCs) can be classified as a correctional setting; some are truly an alternative learning environment. Often the courts are responsible for ALC creation, making mandatory school attendance part of a juvenile probationer's adjudication. (Massachusetts is one state I came across implementing alternative sentencing programs with expressive arts components.) For example, an exhibit of art about family violence allows a juvenile probationer or detainee to engage in dialogue with the community on the issue without divulging confidential information.

Collaborative projects can bring voices, struggles, and dreams into the public spaces that can typically silence or exclude. Creativity, exhibits, and publications, are just some examples that can create ways for individuals to engage, question, and maybe attempt to transform the very social structures that lead to high rates of incarceration. When people share with others their feelings of fear, anguish, and despair, their power to act for change is released.

The arts have the ability to connect people to themselves, their culture, and their communities. These connections are fostered by developing individuality and confidence through creative activities, and by positive social interactions achieved through collaboration. Richmond (2000) notes that 'Giving youth responsibility and expecting accountability is at the core of most successful community youth development initiatives ... young people are learning by doing, and the community and its youth are experiencing positive ripple effects' (p. 24).

'One learns as well or better by doing as reading and listening. Education is not only a function of books, but a function of experience and connecting what one reads and hears by ongoing observation and experiences' (Delgado, 2006, p. 48).

The United Nations International Children's Fund (UNICEF) encourages the participation of marginalized children, and advocates for the active involvement of youth in projects directly affecting their wellbeing. Two examples include:

1 The Arctic Rose Foundation's Messy Book Program is a daily after-school, culture-specific art program for youth in grades 5–12, supporting Northern Inuit, First Nations (Aboriginal), and Métis youth, with Indigenous-led, culturally relevant projects. The program uses a combination of art, non-clinical art-writing therapy, movement, music, digital technology, and drama to connect with culture and promote mental health in a safe space.
2 Voices Unbroken, a non-profit organization, based in New York, U.S.A., is a program for youth providing creative writing self-expression workshops in jails, prisons, and juvenile detention centers '... dedicated to providing workshops for under-heard members of community, primarily youth 12–24.'

> Teens report that reading their poetry is a way to vent their feelings, and hearing poems by their peers puts their own lives in perspective. We make writing a game. These young people have been neglected and abused and are very private about their lives. We are teaching them how to write about that and about love, friendship, goals and dreams. It's about getting them to tap into emotions they may have not wanted to talk about before...learning how to write is more about their sense of self.
>
> (Retrieved August 1, 2024 from voicesunbroken.org/index.html)

Empowerment Theory and Peer Education

Attending a conference titled 'It's Not Too Late' organized by the University of Victoria's Centre for Youth & Society, it was refreshing to hear a more *current* view on youth development as to how positive factors in adolescents' lives help them overcome risks they may face. Keynote speaker, Dr. Marc Zimmerman from the University of Michigan, gave a presentation on his research focusing on adolescent health and what he referred to as 'empowerment theory.' His work involved the measurement and analysis of adolescent resiliency for risks associated with alcohol and drug use, violent behavior, and school failure. These factors are examined in terms of developmental transitions and longitudinal models of change. Empowerment theory stems from 'positive psychology,' whereby the focus is on an individual's assets (these include their family and community).

Where traditional interventions involve doing this *for* youth, empowerment interventions involve participation *with* youth. The techniques provide opportunities for adolescents to engage, develop, and to practice pro-social skills in various settings. The three components of psychological empowerment include: intrapersonal (feeling), interpersonal (critical thinking), and behavioral (actions). Zimmerman reported that alternative services such as community programs provided teens with concrete places for social development and an alternative model to reduce risk factors such as violent behavior.

Zimmerman's research supports what many community educators have learned by professional practice—that by providing a supportive and nurturing environment where adolescents can learn and practice new skills, we empower them (Cross, 2004; Heath, Soep, & Roach, 1998). Optimal programs are youth-driven whereby young people learn social skills and receive support needed to respond to challenges they are facing. Through success in dealing with current challenges they can build a foundation for healthy, productive, and fulfilling lives in the future. Brian Goldfarb (2002) speaks to the importance of visual art projects that engage youth in peer education. He writes that peer education has been a central component of critical pedagogy and liberal education reform initiatives since the 1960s. It is an approach based 'on the view that the educational process, and young people's sense of political engagement and power, is enriched when young people assume pedagogical roles among their peers' (p. 111).

Richmond (2000) notes that 'Giving youth responsibility and expecting accountability is at the core of most successful community youth development initiatives ... young people are learning by doing; the community and its youth are experiencing positive ripple effects' (p. 24). Psychologist Jack Kornfield (2008) has said that when we bring respect to those around us, we open a channel to their own goodness. When children and teens experience someone who respects and values them, it gives them the ability to admire themselves and others.

Community Art Education for Youth 'At Risk'

The term 'at risk' and 'delinquent' label a segment of the population deemed disenfranchised or dispossessed. It is important for me to share with readers my caution about the potential harm that can be done to those assigned these labels. Having said this, I am also sensitive to the need for certain organizations that recognize the economic and political importance of using the term for fundraising efforts.

I was contracted to set up a community organization targeting 'at-risk' adolescents in Vancouver. The program originated in Montreal, Quebec, and in 1999, received a one million dollar Millennium Grant. I visited Vancouver high schools introducing the program and became familiar with many alternative schools. This program assists young people whose lives have been affected by violence. It is unique in using photography and writing to raise awareness of violence as a social problem. My own involvement with writing and drawing helped me as a teenager to define myself and continues to be a presence in my life. Having a degree in fine arts and a background working in various community organizations, it was an exciting and challenging proposition to bring the Montreal model to Vancouver, and to set up a West Coast non-profit program.

The Leave Out Violence Program

> *Violence robs your soul. Violence threatens your life. With violence, you always have to look behind you. You can beat violence with love, friendship and peace. School tells me what I can't do, but in the Leave Out Violence program, they tell me what I can do. They give kids the mentality to want to change the world for the better... I'm glad to be a part of it.*
>
> (Anonymous)

In 2000, I negotiated an arrangement with Langara College to use facilities there. We offered a place for teens to gather in a classroom and were given access to the journalism department's two small (unused) photo labs to process film, print photographs, discuss issues of importance to the youth, and to write about these issues. Equipped with donated point and shoot cameras, a supply of black and white film, chemistry and enlarging paper, pens and notebooks, teens focused on three themes: The causes of youth violence; the impact on all of our lives; and possible ways we can eliminate it.

Teens were referred by teachers, social workers, and sometimes their probation officers; but participation was voluntary. For the first intake, 20 teens were selected and met after school at Langara College twice a week for two semesters to learn photography and creative writing. Upon successful completion (the group decision was 80 per cent class attendance), they were awarded the College's Certificate of Completion at our spring graduation ceremony where photographic images and writings were exhibited. Families, friends, and community members were invited to attend. Still in operation two decades later, the Vancouver program's continuing success affirms my belief in the potential of programs that enrich people's lives, and in particular art programs that lead to positive social change and provide a voice for these young people.

The Mission Statement:

> It's more than just a [photojournalism] program. It's a community for young people whose lives have been affected by violence. Leave Out Viiolence gives them the support, sense of purpose and skills they need to reject negative, aggressive behavior... then work proactively to stamp out violence in our communities. This impacts both the youth and 'decision makers' across racial, cultural, socio-economic and generational borders.
>
> *Why do I write? I write because it takes me right out of my physical self and into my subconscious. It takes me away from wherever I am and can put me wherever I want to go. It's creativity and imagination. It is one of the best things for expanding your mind ... when you are depressed or trying to get over something, if you write to yourself about it or get it out in poetry or something, it helps so much to just get rid of that bad feeling right away. Reading your writing out loud is also so healing in some ways. If you feel comfortable telling someone something out loud sometimes you feel so great afterwards. It's like a free and magic release of some sort. Why write? Write for yourself. Write to feel good about yourself, to be happy and creative. Emotions are released and expressed. No more holding in terrible thoughts.*
>
> (Anonymous)

Projects encouraged critiquing of not only personal experiences, but those of peers, families, and society in general. It is important to mention the program's success was achieved with the support of the teens, their schools, and community. This success eventually led to the program being funded by various community and corporate grants. Project structure and implementation is provided by adults, but the program's success relies on its participants' interest and involvement.

In an issue of *Monday Magazine* (November 30–December 6, 2006) in an article titled 'Healing words: More than just entertainment, storytelling also offers a path to wellness', writer Sarah Gignac reported that a former Leave Out Violence teacher had found this to be one of the most challenging and rewarding projects she had ever been involved with. 'The program not only gets youths dealing with their problems by writing about them, it also provides them with new skills and confidence in themselves' (2006, p. xi).

By taking art education to the community, we understand a place and role for art beyond the classroom and the gallery/museum (Cross, 2004; Becker, 1996). Through my professional experience setting up this non-profit program, I can attest to the benefits of after-school programs that encourage critical examinination of society in general, and communities in particular, through creative art activities. It also provided me with the opportunity to advance a causes I feel strongly about—engaging young people whose voices are under-represented in society in seeking arts-based solutions to social problems, and the power of art for healing through trauma.

Although programs can act as therapeutic tools for some participants, they can also trigger emotional responses that need to be immediately addressed on a professional level. Workshop facilitators should be prepared for these occurrences and notify the youth's professional team if they are in school or an institutional facility when and if the occasion necessitates.

Think of Us, an organization based in the U.S.A., is 'working to transform the child welfare system and improve outcomes for millions of children and families with lived experiences in the child welfare system'. Their website lists the following trigger and content warnings: physical and sexual violence; emotional and verbal abuse; drug and alcohol abuse; eating disorders; suicide and self-harm; mental health and mental illness; racism/ableism; homophobia; transphobia; and Islamophobia (see thinkofus.org, retrieved January 13, 2025).

> *Maybe violence is [a response] to feeling so frustrated that you're not getting what you need in the world ... youth-driven projects help them in seeking for a new way to identify.*
>
> (personal communication, 2008).

Westhaven-Elmhurst Community Recreation Association (WECRA)

One year prior to accepting the contract at the correctional facility, I implemented a research project to investigate the role of art and education at a community setting for teens. The site chosen, WECRA, is a non-profit organization that has been providing services in the borough of Notre Dame des Grace (N.D.G.) (Montreal) for over 40 years. WECRA has a rich and vibrant history. I was born in this community. Built on a background of social inclusion and community engagement, it has catered to the needs of children of all ages in N.D.G. and surrounding areas.

Community-Engaged Learning with University Students

In 2003, I invited my undergraduate students to start a new teen art program for WECRA's youth. The center did not have a teen art program, although there was a weekly teen drop-in night. The project took place over the course of six weeks. A video recorder was used and on hand, and during that time I kept a journal to record notes and comments. Reviewing my journal observations, I noted that the center was highly regarded by the teens, providing them with a safe and supportive environment to socialize. Comments from the youth participants indicate their comfort and appreciation:

> *It's some place where a teen or any kind of kid can have lots of fun, and if you are in some kinda trouble, it's not like going to a youth worker.*
>
> *It's a place where I can come and meet my friends and this facility provides you with the space to do pretty much what you like to do. I like to play ball. I've made friends here.*

When asked what he learned at Westhaven that he didn't or couldn't learn at home or in school, one teen responded:

> *I learned how to respect people, the other teens' cultures and everything. This is a multicultural center and I learned how to deal with problems and how to keep my cool ... certain things, you know. I just turned 18 last week and I am now an adult and I would like to volunteer here at the center.*
>
> (Personal interview, March 2004)

The informality of this community setting allow for in-depth and flexible adult-teen relationships. After-school time should not be more school; it should provide teens with a different space and experience. Observations included:

1. A mix of young and older teens; some had difficulties in school (not wanting to attend) or trouble at home (abuse issues); difficulty 'fitting in' school was prevalent, with a need for a safe place to express themselves.
2. First Night: Getting together with the undergraduate students and teens at the center to discuss and come to a decision on a project that also could be used as a pilot program for the center to use as a funding source. Youth agreed to be involved in every step of the art night, including the design of a logo. Ideas included: bringing in guest speakers, having a video on hand to record progress. The evening launch, with food provided, started with Paula's spoken word, as she distributed copies of her zines. A volunteer who was studying acting, directing, and film showed us a film she had made when she was 16 years old. The idea, she said, came from a conversation she had with her dad about how adults see teenagers. She said that after 8 hours of interviews edited down to 20 minutes: '*I didn't think I'd get so much from interviewing people my own age – I saw different perspectives ... a girl at 16 who is pregnant has a different perspective on life than someone who isn't pregnant.*' (verbatim)

   (The group expressed an interest in the prospect of interviewing each other to find out how they feel about adults, and how they think adults feel about them.)
3. Social Learning Structure: Program must be a product of mutual effort and be of interest in order to succeed. Youth participation is a key piece of positive youth development, and perhaps the most challenging environment for facilitators. Activities that empower adolescents to participate in decision-making that affects their lives, and to take action on issues they care about. We need to link leadership training with decision-making, and social justice with social change. The curriculum methodology and the social learning structure are opposite poles, counter-balancing each other, and providing a safe haven for adolescents to freely create. Although it may be thought of as a formal structure, the

framework of the art program and the social learning structure (even though it can appear to be informal) is the affecting portion of the program for self-expression.

4 Jonathan reports that he attended a henna workshop with a couple of other Asian boys '*... we put Chinese words on our bodies ... I didn't even know what they [words] meaned*'. They were not told by the youth worker what the symbols stood for—this could have turned into an interesting experience for everyone involved ... be 'culturally aware' when presenting to a group ... and if possible, learn and listen for information from the real cultural informants— in their presence ... 'Chinese words' could have been researched as a start to the workshop.

Note: Concordia University Art Education students decided to continue the program. All interviews (teens and program staff) were videotaped; written permission obtained from all involved. A copy was given to the executive director for fundraising efforts.

(Carol Cross, journal entries, 2004)

Conclusion

Not only do adolescents need to be part of the discussions on effective programming but they could also benefit from 'therapeutic' interventions that provide empathetic and attentive assistance. The presence of mentoring and caring adults in programs for youth can provide a natural community support system. Such programs provide productive outlets for young people. Successful community development programs for youth are adapted, not replicated, from other programs, and the most effective ones are those developed in response to specific needs.

The sociocultural approach holds promise for expanding the theory and practice of education, particularly in giving voice to the rich perspectives that learners and instructors bring to the learning environment. Community programs, therefore, can act as learning organizations and continue to provide a safe environment to further support young people. This is especially important in the case of detained youth who sometimes begin to structure their identity around the label 'delinquent'—the effect being future criminal behaviors, diminished employment prospects and educational opportunities, and the receipt of a new label: one of society's 'undesirables'.

Numerous research projects have recorded the impact on students in 'high poverty' and urban settings. It is a common misconception that only 'disadvantaged' teens need help; I have experienced teens from affluent neighborhoods who could easily be labeled 'disadvantaged'.

Multicultural issues must be carefully and sensitively handled, to avoid setting up a voyeuristic and/or tokenistic mindset (Stuhr, 1994).

References

Becker, C. (1996). *Zone of Contention: Essays on art institutions, gender, and anxiety*. Albany, NY: State University New York Press.

Congdon, K.G. (1984). Art education in a jail setting. A personal perspective. *Art Education*, 37(2), 10–11.

Cross, C. (2004). Stepping out: Finding one's place and transforming space through art. *BCATA Journal for Art Teachers*, 45(1), 12–16.

Delgado, M. (2006). *New Frontiers for Youth Development in the Twenty-First Century. Revitalizing and broadening youth development*. New York: Columbia University Press.

Eisner, E.W. (1999). *Beyond the School: Community and institutional partnerships in art education.* EDS, NAEA.
Gignac, S. (2006). Healing words: More than just entertainment, storytelling also offers a path to wellness. *Monday Magazine* (Vancouver Island community newspaper).
Giroux, H.A. (2003). Public pedagogy and the politics of resistance: Notes on a critical theory of educational struggle. *Educational Philosophy & Theory*, 35, 5–16.
Goldfarb, B. (2002). *Visual Pedagogy: Media cultures in and beyond the classroom.* Durham, NC: Duke University Press.
Heath, S.B., Soep, E., & Roach, A. (1998). Living the arts through language-learning: A report on community-based youth organizations. *Americans for the Arts Monographs*, 2.
Kornfeld, P. (1997). *Cellblock Visions: Prison art in America.* Princton, NJ: Princeton University Press.
Kornfield, J. (2008). *The wise heart: A guide to the universal teachings of Buddhist psychology.* New York: Random House.
Lorde, A. (1995). *The Black Unicorn.* New York: W.W. Norton.
McLaughlin, M. (2000). *Community Counts: How youth organizations matter for youth development.* Washington, DC: Public Education Network. Retrieved September 25, 2009 from www.publiceducation.org/cgi/bin/download-manager/publications/p/72.asp.
Richmond, J. (2000). New partnerships and new systems: Supporting young people's growth and job readiness. *CYD Journal*, 1, 20–25.
Stuhr, P.L. (1994). Multicultural art education and social reconstruction. *Studies in Art Education*, 35(3), 171–178.
Sullivan, G. (2005). *Art Practice as Research: Inquiry in the visual arts.* Thousand Oaks, CA: Sage.

Chapter 5

The Projects

Introduction

Chapter 5 continues the discussion of youth-driven projects, contributing to the ongoing process of understanding the culture and subculture of youth correctional facilities and the role of the expressive arts in reducing stress, making the experience of incarceration more productive, and ultimately, reducing recidivism. I discuss the therapeutic benefits of creating art—mental health is fostered, and it encourages adolescent identity and self-confidence.

Chapter 4 discussed my experiences as a community art educator establishing the Leave Out Violence project. While community art education projects do not *replace* the four settings where adolescents can face multiple risks—the family, the community, their peer environment, and school (Noam, Winner, Rhein, & Molad, 1996)—youth-driven programs do have the potential to provide an important element to 'at-risk' teens: a safe place that provides an alternative environment to construct positive peer world relationships that may be missing in their lives (Chase, 2008). Leave Out Violence youth gained skills in photography, writing, and leadership; and exercised a community relationship building approach. They also came to discuss feelings and unload the stresses of their personal lives in a supportive environment. I believe this environment can be replicated within the confines of juvenile detention centers.

Prison Art Programs

Too little has been addressed about the nature or the relevance of prison art programs. It has been said that imagination is freedom even behind prison bars.

In this chapter, I describe the projects I introduced with incarcerated male and female adolescents: a magazine (*Inside-Out Magazine*); wall art (The Mural Project), a self-directed computer media and visual art program (The Sunday Art + Design Group), and *The Outside Guide*, a youth participatory action research (YPAR) project. The research group as a whole expressed the hope that future incarcerated teens could also benefit from these projects.

Juvenile detainees are protected by strong confidentiality restrictions. Faces cannot appear and full names cannot be used, but they can use their first names, initials or sign their works with a pseudonym or 'anonymous'. Although they cannot be identified in any way, artistic work does put a 'face' on the inmates. Even though they remain in some ways anonymous, the constructive items they produced can show a positive aspect of these young people—humanizing them and showcasing their talents. Adolescents, like the rest of us,

DOI: 10.4324/9781003534082-5

seldom voluntarily pursue activities from which they receive little or no satisfaction. This is an important first factor, one that is supported by my doctoral research, and that of other institutions such as one in a U.K. penitentiary for adult males.

In *The Special Unit, Barlinnie Prison: Its evolution through its art*, Carrell and Laing (1982) suggest that had the arts been programmed as an 'education pursuit' not one of the inmates would have agreed to participate, as this would have been viewed with the same distaste with which many inmates had come to associate their previous educational experiences. They state that all prisoners had arrived at the unit from long periods of solitary confinement 'from outbursts of violent behaviors and years of suspicion, hatred and distrust ... [C]reativity offered the individual his own pace of self understanding' (p. 92).

A second important factor is that as opposed to the recreational art program that already existed prior to my contract with the juvenile correctional facility, projects were youth-driven. Experiencing the arts in the context of programs for and with them increases the chance that they will find pleasure because there is a great deal of freedom to do whatever they would like to do. Through encouragement, proper instruction, and with artistic tools made available, their creative expression can flourish, allowing them opportunity to create work that is *fearless*, *fresh*, and *innovative.*

Drawings and paintings also became visual records documenting their time, and sometimes reactions, to incarceration. Apart from using art as yet another correctional program, we can discover the value derived from the participatory *process* of artistic creation. Positive social support is associated with improved mental health. *Inside-Out Magazine* provided an outlet for personal expression and social support.

Participating in inmate-initialed endeavors contrasts markedly with taking correctional programs (see Appendix A: A Reflective Letter from a role model reprinted in its entirety.) The following is a brief summary of contributing factors:

- Inmate-initiated endeavors are voluntary as opposed to mandatory, and they concentrate on *personal development* as opposed to character 'correction'.
- They *encourage excellence* as opposed to punishing error.
- They *promote creativity* as opposed to enforcing discipline.
- They impart a strong sense of *ownership* to their participants, *positive feelings* of self-esteem and self-determination often result, a benefit that not only allows for immediate learning but also encourages further exploration, creating an upward-spiraling process of *mental and spiritual growth.*
- *Rehabilitation* is more effectively realized when the person who is being rehabilitated perceives that he or she has a stake in the process. The sense of ownership these endeavors impart upon participants coalesces with the resultant feelings of self-determination and together they fuel further learning, dignity, and decorum.
- Although there can be a different statement expressed in each individual submission (*Inside-Out Magazine*), the overall representation is one of *contrite hope and self-realization.*

Proposing Prison Programs

Addressing the issue of proposing new projects or programs when working within the confines of a correctional facility relies solely upon allowing an outsider (me) to instigate and encourage the inmates/clients—in my case, adolescents. Proposals need to be submitted to the Director of Operations (Warden) for final approval—they are responsible for the overall operation of the facility and have the power to sanction or veto any request. In my case, the Director was a strong supporter of the magazine project. This project would extend beyond the walls of 'corrections'—copies of the magazine were displayed at a conference and held in the community for social service agencies in order to network with other organizations. Conference attendees included court workers, probation officers, youth workers, psychologists, and correctional officers.

The Collective Voice – Producing a Prison Publication

The poet, essayist, feminist, and equal rights activist Audre Lorde wrote that when we speak we are afraid our words will not be heard nor welcomed, but when we are silent we are still afraid, so it is better to speak.

My four objectives for starting a magazine for and with incarcerated teens were simple: 1) to provide youths the opportunity to express themselves in a creative fashion; 2) to do something positive and creative with their talents and their time; 3) to showcase their artistic works and crafts; 4) and to obtain for these youth some language rights to free speech and individual expression while incarcerated. Our mandate was to publish a magazine 'by the residents with its sole purpose for the enjoyment and enlightenment of the residents, their friends and family, the staff, and any other interested parties.'

This project was designed to help the youth *enhance* their existing developmental assets, which can have a powerful influence on adolescent behavior—both protecting young people from problem behaviors and promoting positive behaviors. The developmental assets that the project was intended to build are the artistic skills that I believe most youths already possess. Professionally printed in color four times per year, the magazine highlighted their talents by providing a venue where teens could display their self-directed visual art and writing skills, along with their arts and craft projects.

In a retrospective issue, the Editorial Board found the following five distinct themes and/or recurring topics: personal issues (family and friends); emotional and traumatic issues (anger, death, violence); substance misuse, prevention, and peer education; social issues (juvenile justice system and 'doing time'); critical self-reflection, choices, and the desire for change.

In summary, the magazine project provided opportunities for teens from a variety of culturally specific backgrounds to do something positive and creative with their talents and their time 'inside'. The writing and art created for each issue not only focused on each individual's story, but also testified to their inner strength and survival instincts that allowed them to move beyond personal challenges. It also benefited the teens by granting them permission to say things they wouldn't otherwise have been allowed to. They gained a greater measure of rights to free speech and individual expression through their writing and art projects, and gave readers a glimpse into the teens' lives with the hope that this would lead to understanding as to why they do what they do and what it means to them.

Some teens reported that engaging in art programs provided them with time away from their stressful housing units. They would often enter the room and unload negative feelings; they felt comfortable and safe enough to process their feelings about unit regulations and experiences with their peers. An excerpt from a teen, titled 'Reality on the inside', for

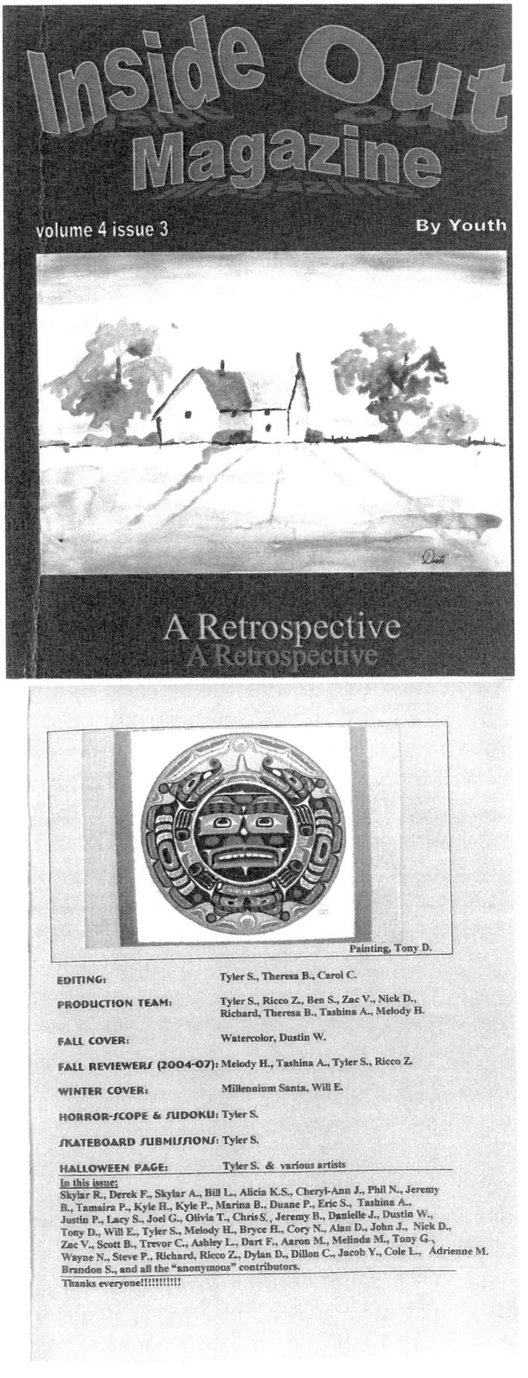

Painting, Tony D.

EDITING: Tyler S., Theresa B., Carol C.

PRODUCTION TEAM: Tyler S., Ricco Z., Ben S., Zac V., Nick D., Richard, Theresa B., Tashina A., Melody H.

FALL COVER: Watercolor, Dustin W.

FALL REVIEWERS (2004-07): Melody H., Tashina A., Tyler S., Ricco Z.

WINTER COVER: Millennium Santa, Will E.

HORROR-SCOPE & SUDOKU: Tyler S.

SKATEBOARD SUBMISSIONS: Tyler S.

HALLOWEEN PAGE: Tyler S. & various artists

In this issue:
Skylar R., Derek F., Skylar A., Bill L., Alicia K.S., Cheryl-Ann J., Phil N., Jeremy B., Tamaira P., Kyle H., Kyle P., Marina B., Duane P., Eric S., Tashina A., Justin P., Lacy S., Joel G., Olivia T., Chris S., Jeremy B., Danielle J., Dustin W., Tony D., Will E., Tyler S., Melody H., Bryce H., Cory N., Alan D., John J., Nick D., Zac V., Scott B., Trevor C., Ashley L., Dart F., Aaron M., Melinda M., Tony G., Wayne N., Steve P., Richard, Ricco Z., Dylan D., Dillon C., Jacob Y., Cole L., Adrienne M. Brandon S., and all the "anonymous" contributors.

Thanks everyone!!!!!!!!!!!

Figure 5.1 Inside-Out Magazine, A Retrospective, cover top and credits publication in the magazine gives readers some insight to an imprisoned experience and shares the reality for youth living in a correctional institution:

> *At night, I sit by my window and daydream about the real world.*
>
> *I'm still in reality here, but it's different; I'm so restricted of anything and everything. I can't get a job like I used to be able to. I have to ask to clear my plate of food. If one piece of cutlery is not returned after a meal, we all get our rooms ripped apart, we're then strip-searched and locked until it's found. Some days I feel like an animal locked in a cage. I find myself gazing at the ceiling and not even knowing what I'm feeling. Pain, ashamed, sadness, anger, loneliness! I don't know, it's all bundled up and it hurts deep inside my soul. I know every day my criminal past has left an emotional scar that will forever last.*
>
> (Anonymous)

The project morphed into more than just a 'juvie' magazine. Our first issue, a stapled and photocopied slim issue of reflective writing and pencil drawings, grew in size and quality to include color photographs of the teens' artistic work. The first issue's cover showcased our first painted mural; and 10 pages consistently grew to 84 pages, providing a forum for 'residents' to write, reflect, and discuss matters of concern to them, share their creativity, and build a *peer supportive link* among the young people living in the four secure units.

The reflective writing and creation of art reflected self-directed initiatives within the subculture of incarcerated teens, had an overall message of personal transformation, and demonstrated a desire for healing of self and their peers. By collectively engaging in this youth-driven project, sharing personal stories and information, the teens again succeeded in reaching beyond the walls of the juvenile justice system. Approximately 80 copies of each quarterly issue were professionally bound and color printed, and shipped back to me for distribution. Each teen that submitted work received one copy and two copies were placed on each unit in a special non-breakable wall mount for everyone to read, along with a poster announcing the deadline for the next issue. A copy was placed in the reception area for all visitors to the center, one in the arts & crafts room, the center's school classroom, and another in the correctional facility's staff room. A copy was placed as reading material on a table in the clinical reception area for the youth who were waiting to see the nurse, the psychologist or psychiatrist, and another copy was mailed to Youth Forensics Psychiatric Services. Although not all staff support the idea of a magazine for and by the youth, the Director of Operations (Warden) who had initially granted permission after reviewing our first issue, requested an additional 15 copies be printed for distribution to *all probation officers* directly involved in supervising and working with discharged youth. This project provided an outlet for personal expression and social support. Young participants (maybe for the first time in their lives) are empowered—they can possess a sense of worth within a system that is designed to 'correct' behaviors by stripping them of their adolescent identity and limiting their rights. In summary, by supporting projects by and for youth, we adults are telling them that we believe in them, we value their skills and appreciate what they *can* be. Even though I engaged regularly with the teens, I could never begin to describe, let alone speak for or understand, what it might be like to live in a locked, confined environment. When program participants have the opportunity to portray their experiences through various art forms, they often gain insights and reveal them through the language of art. For those who are less articulate, who learn in different ways, or who have different cultural backgrounds, it can be a most useful means of engaging in reflection and analysis of their time in a juvenile facility. In this restrictive environment, art offers them a 'voice'.

Correctional Services Canada (CSC) continues not to recognize the need to provide special housing, programming, or other services for younger prisoners. Their official position is that programs available to all prisoners can be *adapted* to meet the needs of younger prisoners, but I disagree; programming should not only be about age, but should also be culturally appropriate and staffed accordingly.

Mentorship: LINC, EDGE, and Patrick (Pat) R.

Appendix A is a rather lengthy quote by Patrick (Pat) R. who accepted my invitation to provide his insights into the magazine project for my doctoral thesis. He has provided a well-articulated argument that warrants inclusion—all nine pages of it—and is reprinted in its entirety with his permission once again. Pat became involved with the *Inside-Out Magazine* project in its initial stages. I met him when the correctional facility made an arrangement with a group known by the acronym LINC (Long-term Inmates Now in the Community). Members of this group were granted permission under the guidance of the center's chaplain to provide a series of workshop/seminars for the teens. The program called EDGE (Everyone Deserves Growth & Empowerment), focuses on developing life-skills and crime prevention. Designed for youth in schools and/or community settings, the program was developed and delivered by members of LINC.

Pat was interested in my idea to start a magazine for and by incarcerated teens, as he had prior experience as writer, editor, and publisher of *Out of Bounds*, a prison magazine at William Head Penitentiary. I invited Pat to come to the custody center again as a guest speaker to meet with teens involved in a group program I facilitated called YVIP (Youth Violence Intervention Program), and he decided to give a talk on restorative justice. The teens responded enthusiastically to his talk. Pat was interested in continuing to provide support to the teens on a volunteer basis and met with the custody center's Volunteer Coordinator, but was denied permission to re-enter the facility due to his history of incarceration. He remained committed to the magazine project and not only provided valuable support for this new venture but also contributed articles to our magazine that sent a message of hope and encouragement to the teens. I asked Pat if he would be interested in sharing his experiences with *Out of Bounds*. He agreed to contribute his views on the subject of art education and incarceration. The full text appears in Appendix A. To summarize:

1 Empowerment comes from actions taken through experiential learning:

> *Experiential learning is an important aspect of any endeavor. We learn best by doing. Didactic programs offered by correctional institutions often fail miserably because they involve less than impartial instructors (prison personnel) lecturing less than enthusiastic participants (coerced inmates) with a premise that is as controversial as it is demeaning (you're defective, we can fix you). Rehabilitation is more effectively realized when the person who is being rehabilitated perceives that he or she has a stake in that process. With inmate-initiated projects that perception is a self-evident outcome. The sense of ownership these endeavors impart upon their participants coalesces with the resultant feelings of self-determination and together they fuel further learning, dignity, and decorum.*

2 Self-esteem is the foundation for progress:

Without doubt, the singular most significant altered attribute would have to be the higher self-esteem and its concomitant increase in feelings of self-worth that one experiences from having his or her writing or art published. And perhaps the most ostensive opportunity a prison publication provides is as a venue for disseminating discontent, an experience, which can actually alleviate some of the frustrations that prisoners often accumulate from not having a voice. These frustrations, if they are not expressed in an appropriate manner, can lead to destructive thoughts and aberrant behavior.

3 Praising the publication, *Inside-Out Magazine,* Pat observes:

The message in Inside-Out*, a publication that is by and for youth in custody, emanates from the writing and art published in the magazine. The message is one of emancipation. Writing (as well as producing other art forms) is a liberating sentiment. The opportunity to voice one's concerns and opinions in a prison publication, combined with the educational experience that comes from learning how to write effectively, in an objective manner, speaks to the psychological and intellectual well-being touched upon earlier in this article. If prisoners believe that they can make positive changes, their incarceration becomes less troublesome in both scope and duration. If people in custody can learn to accomplish things for the common good of their little microcosm of society, a microcosm replete with an abundance of hate, anger, violence and selfishness, then in a sense they are liberating themselves from those otherwise negative constraints.*

In Retrospection ... the Writing

Over the years since its inception, *Inside-Out Magazine* morphed into more than a 'juvie' magazine. The first issue of 10 pages gradually grew to 84 pages, providing a forum for teen residents to write, reflect, and discuss matters of concern to them, share their creativity, and build a peer *supportive link* among the young people living in the custody units. The reflective writing and creation of art reflect self-directed initiatives within the subculture of incarcerated teens, with an overall message of personal transformation and a desire for healing of self and their peers. By collectively engaging in this youth-driven project, sharing personal stories and information, the teens succeeded in reaching *beyond* the walls of the juvenile justice system. Magazine covers celebrated our latest painted mural (we completed nine), and there were original pencil-drawn comic strips, a 'horror-scope', quotes, and special sections of the magazine highlighting events held in the custody center.

As Pat R. states, not only did his involvement with the prison publication *Out of Bounds* help him survive a long prison sentence, it also helped prisoners, prison staff, and the public gain insight into what it means to be incarcerated. Writing helped him understand and express his emotions. It also enabled him to understand some of the complicated social issues that had led to his taking another man's life many years earlier. Writing can be an important educational experience, a process leading to character development. The educational experience that comes from publishing a prison magazine is unique and profoundly valuable.

Horror-scopes

Libra (Sept 24 – Oct 23)

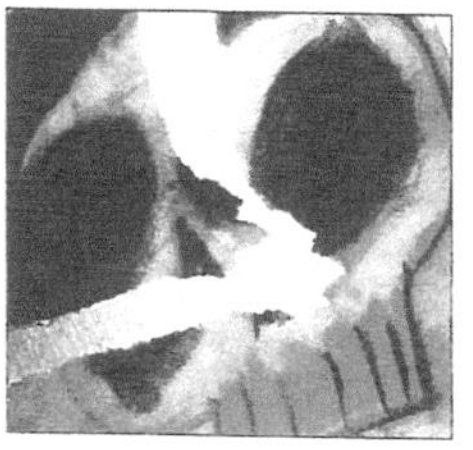

Unfortunately, the moon, sun, and earth are lined up perfectly, which could possibly mean 24 hour lockdowns will be passed out to you like candy.

Scorpio (Oct 24 – Nov 22)

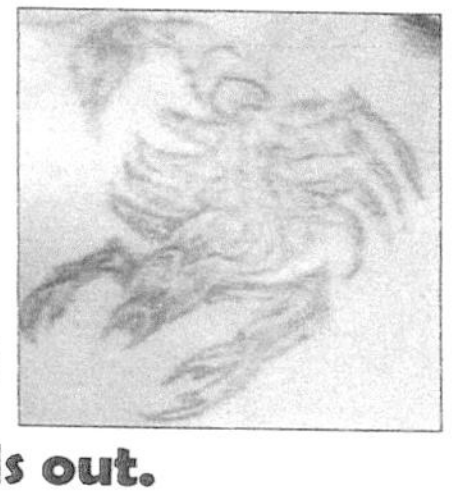

After a reading of the stars, it was found out Mr. Yagger possibly lost more hair than usual and could drop you to a level one-meals out.

Sagittarius (Nov 23 – Dec 21)

Everyone wants to be a critic. Everyone wants to have their say. This could be you. But a new instated law brought to us by VYCC says no one cares.

Capricorn (Dec 22 – Jan 20)

Pluto and Uranus have collided so get rid of all contraband because they will probably suspect you as the culprit and rooms will be tossed.

Figure 5.2 'Horror-scopes'

The majority of detained youth submitted creative art and/or reflective writing to *Inside-Out Magazine*. Walking through the housing units, I sometimes would get a folded up piece of paper handed to me to stick in my back pocket. Teens released prior to distribution were mailed a copy. Once the magazine was sent to the Ministry's (government) printer, the teens frequently asked me if it had arrived. When I showed up on the units with the latest issue in hand, their excitement was evident. Everyone milled around me excited, laughing at some of the images. D. asked me if he can have a copy for his mother and I hand him one to send to her. Will it affect her? And in what way—I'll never know. I only know that they appear proud and happy—many thanked me for my hard work but I reminded them that without their submissions there would be no magazine.

> *I've taken my work home with me—I slept little ... there are constant thoughts, I will relate: our latest issue is the most successful to date—more than half of the teens have participated—comments of self-esteem are positive and high. One teen has related this to the psychiatrist in a session—they're afraid he'll try and hang himself while in city cells waiting for court. I recommend video court, but they say they can't do video court (at the correctional facility)—they say his P.O. [probation officer] has given up.*
>
> *The psychiatrist's comment in the medical file reads: 'the teen in question takes pleasure in being part and should continue being involved in the Inside-Out program'. The teen likes to draw and write. He's expressing himself so perfectly in writing –but the Director of Programs wants me to spend less time on the magazine project. He has no interest or understanding of the power of art for self-expression here ... what is the system doing to or for our future generation?*
>
> (Carol Cross, journal entry, 2008)

The magazine project was a successful vehicle that engaged those individuals (clinical personnel or otherwise) serving the needs of these youth. They read about the *thoughts*, the *feelings*, and the *hopes* of these young people, in powerful examples of their personal stories, and viewed the artistic skill created and exhibited in the magazine by the youth they served. I have witnessed the benefits of designing programs that see the *potential* of incarcerated youth as *contributors*, instead of bearing the label of 'delinquent troublemakers'.

I conclude this section with an example written by A., another frequent contributor. In 'Give Yourself a Chance', A. addresses her peer group and implores them to consider how their *choices* affect the other people in their lives.

> *As I walk through VYCC, I notice most of these youth aren't proud to be. Proud to be serving time, you'd probably rather be out there creating crime. Think about that for a minute or two. Ask yourself 'who can make a change in life?' It could be you! Yeah, I'm sitting here too, but that's not really the point ... you have to tell yourself not to give up and give yourself a chance. Because there's lots out there to embrace ... hang out with your grandparents or bring the kids to the park. If you're*

going to steal a car ... really think about it before you make your final decision. Do you really want to be in here, or out there on a mission? This place is not what you want in life, is it? And tell yourself ... not to give up. If you have a little sister or brother, talk to them, because you shouldn't be here, I shouldn't either. But we made the choice ... now raise your voice and remember to always give yourself a chance.

Young people are, and will continue to be, further traumatized by the 'carceral' experience. When they are given the supports, sense of purpose, and life skills they will need, they will be able to make choices that can improve the quality of their lives, regardless of their past circumstances. Multiple interventions are required to help them navigate and reintegrate successfully into society.

Arts and Crafts versus Youth-driven Projects

The custody center's Arts and Crafts instructor, was also supportive of the *Inside-Out Magazine* project. The magazine project provided a record for the custody center of the Arts and Crafts work she taught in her program. To reiterate—the Arts and Crafts program took place in a design designated room. All the youth-driven programs (except for the painting of murals) took place in the clinical multipurpose room. I had optimistically thought I would have access to the Arts and Crafts room on the weekend (when it was not in use) but was denied because I was a 'non-unionized contractor'.

The Creative Process and Imagery Selection

Tupac is revered by many teens (male and female), and his portrait reminds me of the powerful influence the entertainment industry can have on young people. Tupac would appear as drawings and wood burning crafts in issues of *Inside-Out Magazine*, and arrived as submissions when completed in the teens' Arts and Crafts program. Had there been a wider selection of portraits to choose from in the image box, other teen idols would likely have appeared as subjects. C. explains that a lot of teens favor rap music because they can associate with the artist's lyrics. In an excerpt from, 'It's Just the Way I am', he explains:

A lot of kids use drugs and alcohol to get away from all of their problems in this world. And a lot of people just don't understand us, and even we don't understand ourselves. For those who don't ... it is because they have not been in our shoes or have not seen enough to understand. For example, Eminem raps. It's one way of expressing his anger and like he said in one of his songs he's just telling his life story. I respect him for that. There are a lot of people who don't approve of his singing because they don't understand. A lot of kids like him so much as well as his music because we've been through some of the things he talks about and we understand him—that's why we like rap because we understand it.

The weekend program encouraged participants to learn to design and draw self-portraits. We also provided them with the use of a digital camera and printer. Adolescents for the most part are interested in their physical appearance, especially since there are no mirrors in a correctional facility. In The Sunday Art + Design Group project, teens would photograph each other and download their images onto the computer's Photoshop software—printing their photographs and/or digitally altering their images artistically. In conversation with Theresa Bennett, who co-facilitated The Sunday Art + Design Group, she noted that they eagerly engaged in learning photography, posing for one another and negotiating the compositions. Teens would talk about when to take the photo and insist upon creative ownership—not allowing peers to 'cramp their style'. Theresa would encourage the teens to consider various angles of view and entreat them to not be shy. They would make a copy in order to practice their drawing skills, and sometimes create a self-portrait pencil drawing. This exercise would also provide them with drawing content so they could continue creating art together on their units or in their rooms.

Figure 5.3 C.D., 'Tupac' drawing and wood burning

Figure 5.4 Anonymous, Self-Portrait, Pencil Drawing

The Sunday Art + Design Group

I formed The Sunday Art + Design Group for those teens interested in learning to draw, paint, or explore computer design. The program was available to all teens, and those who elected to join the group were provided with a sketchbook and encouraged to draw and document their artistic ideas while on their living units. When I appeared on a walk-through they would show me their sketchbooks for review and instruction. They would also draw in their sketchbooks in more public areas where other teens on the unit would notice, and often comment, on their artistic skills. Of note, those involved in the Sunday Group never forgot to bring their sketchbooks to class and expressed their appreciation for the privilege of attending. Proud of being part of this group, they were willing to show peers what they had sketched during the week, and were receptive to comments from the group as a whole. I also saw them continuing to work in their sketchbooks in the Arts and Crafts room. I subcontracted Theresa to co-facilitate. She has a strong background in graphic art and design. Those interested in attending the Sunday Group completed the following questionnaire prior to attending:

THE SUNDAY Art + Design GROUP

Name:______________________________ Age: ____

This questionnaire is to give us (Theresa and Carol) ideas on how we can help you with your art making abilities.

1 The weekend art + design program focuses on two areas: **1.** Fine Art **2.** Media Art (working on the computer with design software).

Please **circle** the one (or both) of interest to you.

2 Have you taken art or design in your school or at a community center? (yes or no) If you circled **yes**, underline if this was: drawing, painting, computer art, computer games,

or____ .

____

3 What art making or design skills do you have an interest in learning? (i.e. drawing; painting; photoshop; scanning/computer drawing,etc.)

or...____

4 What objects or things do you like to draw, or have an interest in learning how to draw?

____

____

5 What do you think you would need to improve? i.e. art or design mags/books; videos on artists?

____

6 Are you interested in continuing to develop your art making abilities during the week? (yes or no) if yes, what materials do you need?

____

Thanks!!!

Responses were consistent and positive. For example, question 4: *What objects or things do you like to draw, or have an interest in learning how to draw?* Responses included: landscapes and animals, dragons, serpents and vampires, crosses, faces and people, symmetrical and scientific images, and the remainder wrote 'anything'. Question 6: *Are you interested in continuing to develop your art making abilities during the week? If yes, what materials do you need?* All teens responded 'yes' and requested 'drawing materials' and 'magazines or books' to help achieve this.

Body art was of interest and formed part of the culture of *some* adolescents; many expressed pride in showing off their tattoos. Consequently, Theresa and I brought visual resources to the class. Resources included tattoo magazines and books on the history of body art. I believe that tattoos are more than mere decoration; they are a transformation of the body and therefore *the self*. It is a means of realizing oneself as an individual as it marks the 'self' as different from the 'mass'. The youth spent many hours looking through the books and magazines we provided, and would personalize and sketch some ideas for tattoos they hoped to one day have.

In youth-directed projects I observed a sense of connectedness, collaboration, and inter-activity—participants were enriched by the experience. Art activities must be intrinsically rewarding for youth. I believe today's youth want a voice in shaping their communities and their world, but for that to occur, art programs need to provide engaging ways of *learning* to gain and maintain the attention of young people. Participation can be a critical catalyst for change, having the potential to activate individuals and entire communities (Cross, 2002). Whatever the form, the emphasis on any collaborative project should be on allowing participants to speak for themselves. Art produced in a group should be determined by the participants and the particular circumstances of each situation. Youth-driven programs were contrary to the facility's existing Arts and Crafts program.

The Arts and Crafts instructor, C.M., felt she had little choice but to adapt to the traditional institutional values upheld at the custody center, or risk a reprimand from correctional officers. 'We'd be talked to by the SCO [senior correctional officer] and they would tell me that it's not appropriate. ' C.M. adhered to the center's guidelines and was aware that correctional officers monitored the Arts and Crafts room on a daily basis. The teens had to fit all of their art and woodwork (that they are working on or completed) in a small storage box affixed to the wall. They could only claim their belongings when they are released. Here is an example of one of the projects:

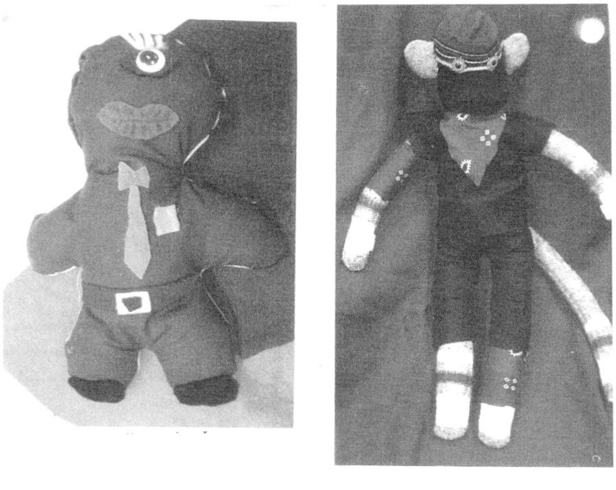

Figure 5.5 Example of sock monkey project, Arts and Crafts Program

The Mural Project

Murals are an art form that demands the collaboration of creative minds to conceptualize the design and produce a large wall painting. Success on a project of this kind also requires a strong adherence to the artistic team as a whole for its production and completion.

Large-scale art initiatives have almost never originated within underserved, underprivileged, visible minority communities. In 2001, I attended a lecture at the University of British Columbia, and was inspired by the work of muralist and art educator Olivia Gude. I share her belief in the potential of large-scale paintings to not only beautify but to also act as a means to *reclaim* public space.

Gude recognized that far from being a preserve, separate from life, art is inherently connected to issues about culture, about human possibility, about justice. Art does not have to address an elite audience or exist solely in museums and galleries. I approached the custody center's Director of Operations with another youth-driven project idea. Although we were not given permission to paint murals on the outside walls of the center, we did gain his approval to paint on the inside walls of the units with the stipulation that we submit original designs and wait for approval before commencing.

Acting as lead artist and talking to the teens for feedback on forming a new group, the decision was welcomed as a positive development. I felt that, prior to the design being submitted to the Director for approval, it must first have the approval of other youths on the units. I honestly never thought we would gain the center's permission to paint murals because many individuals working in 'corrections' view painting on walls as an act of vandalism. I approached a few teens about forming a Mural Group and secured the interest of four teens to work on our first mural. We met on Saturday afternoons (initially in the clinical multi-purpose room to brainstorm design ideas). We would eventually complete nine murals.

A few correctional officers expressed their disapproval of the idea, predicting the murals would be 'marked up' by other teens. But none of our nine murals were ever damaged or marked in any way; in fact, the teens were quick to compliment the designers and always wanted to help the artists while we painted. Most of the murals were painted with acrylic and brushes, but one was completed (with a correctional officer's permission) with the addition of spray-paint art. I believe the youth viewed the murals with communal pride. The 'inside' murals came to be seen 'outside' as they were proudly featured in the *Inside-Out Magazine* and often formed our front cover design. I never heard negative comments from the teens—in fact, after viewing the success of our first mural, other teens soon formed a group on their unit and produced a design that they hoped would be painted.

If a mural was to be painted on a housing unit, all teens on that unit had to approve the design, and then it was submitted to the Director for final approval. Since I always kept a camera on hand in my office, many teens would ask me if I could take their photos in order to send to family members—and they often chose a mural as backdrop.

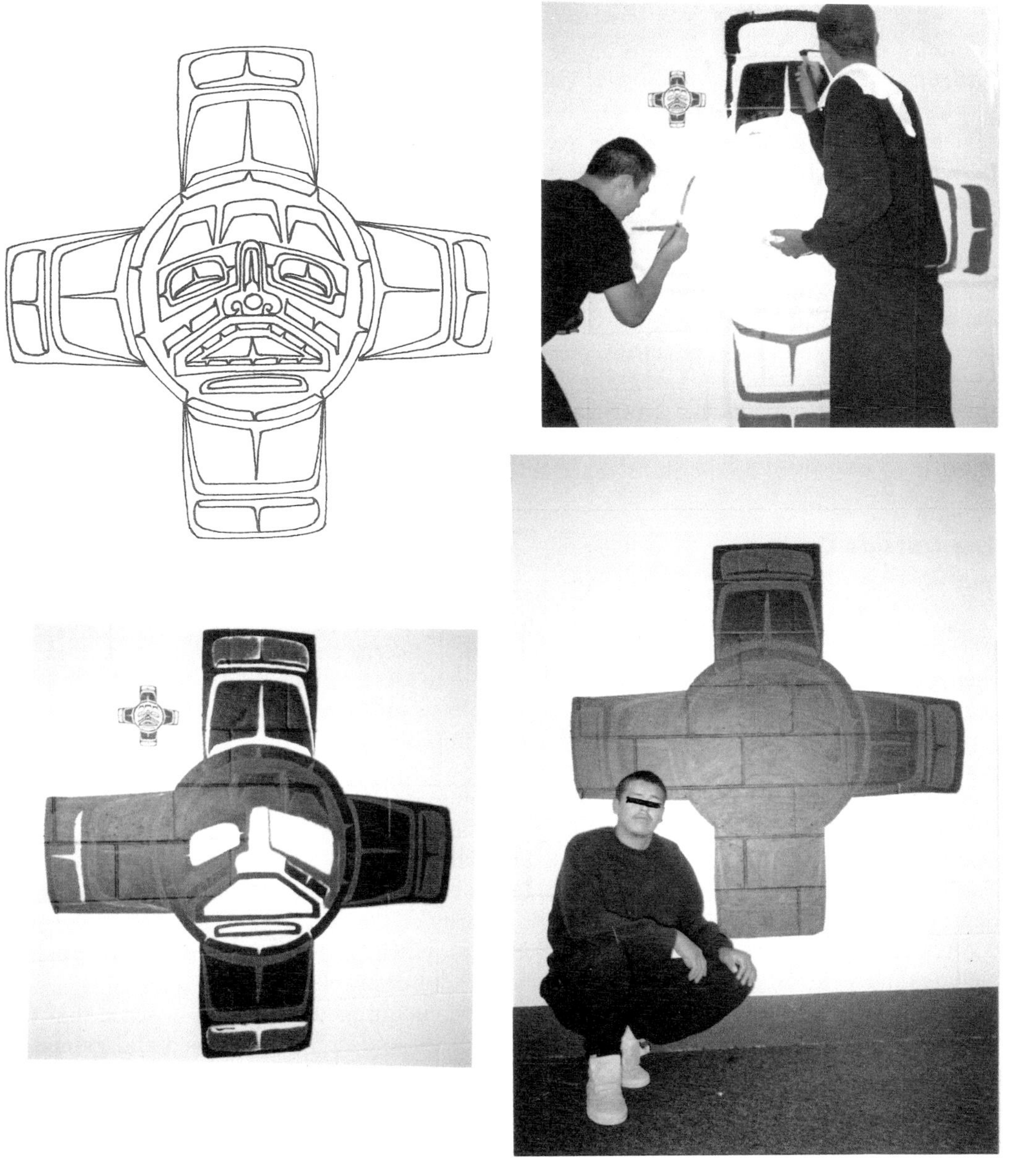

Figure 5.6 C.J. and C.R., Stages in painting mural on Unit 1

Source: Photograph by Carol Cross

Indigenous Art and Design

A book I purchased prior to working at the custody center, *Learning by Designing: Pacific Northwest Coast Native Indian Art*, Volume 2 (2002) was of interest to Aboriginal youth working on their mural designs. The book placed First Nations art within a cultural context and provided differing styles of west coast, north coast, mid coast, and south coast designs. It was an invaluable aid for teens wanting to practice their drawing skills and was frequently passed from one teen to the next. As a matter of cultural sensitivity, I believe a First Nations mural should be designed and painted by Aboriginal youth, although non-aboriginal youth may help with wall layout and painting. In fact, a few Aboriginal teens on the units had learned to draw and carve from family members who were established artists. An interest in traditional designs manifested in other ways—teens would ask me for photocopies of designs to colour during periods of 'lock-down'. *Learning by Designing* was an invaluable resource for me, a non-aboriginal art educator. It was one way of demonstrating the respect I have for Pacific Northwest Coast Native art. By respecting their *culture*, we show respect. It also provided the youth with an educational tool to teach *me* about their cultures as we talked about and researched varying design styles.

The Outside Guide

The Outside Guide, another youth-initiated project, researched community services, education, and other resources (or lack of them) collectively. It provided a unique opportunity for young offenders to form a group to elicit their concerns and insights for themselves with their peers who would soon be released or mandated to community supervision. Male and female offenders worked together on a weekly basis and were instrumental in researching youth-friendly resources in each of their communities, and provided another benefit for many teens who had spent the majority of their youth in correctional facilities and would soon be released. It also afforded youths the opportunity to learn and work with adults, as well as master technical design skills that they could continue to utilize in their communities. The credit page of this portable booklet listed their name and their position (e.g., Production Manager, InDesign Pre-Press, Layout Illustrator, etc.). Especially in the case of detained youth who begin to structure their identity around the label 'delinquent', the effect is often future criminal behavior, diminished employment and educational opportunities, as well as the receipt of a new label: one of society's 'undesirables'.

Consistently throughout the weeks, teens were encouraged to develop a sense that they could have fun *and* learn skills in the creation of art and design. I lobbied and gained the confidence of the center's administration to purchase a new computer and design software for the purpose of teaching production and design skills. This project also acted effectively as a tool for the involved teens to investigate and document resources for youth—resources that were *sanctioned* by them. They reconnected (albeit on the 'inside') with their home communities. This is important for teens who are soon to be *reintegrated* into society. I believe this youth-driven project embraced not only their creative needs, but also provided them with a real sense of accomplishment and a *positive learning experience.*

Whether we are working in an institutional setting (a correctional facility) or in the community sphere, we design educational programs to also improve the ways in which young people *think*. As pointed out by Smith (1989), the field of art education is *predominately* child and youth oriented. The principal aim is the development of the *learners* themselves.

In contrast with highly directed programs where teachers set out a very prescribed series of steps leading to a predetermined outcome, art educators ought to strive to design situations where young people become more skilled so their creative endeavors are realized and achieved. The educational leader (whether that be a coordinator, facilitator, resource advisor, tutor, or coach) may accomplish that aim in various ways depending on their theoretical orientation.

I regard myself as a constructivist educator with a democratic approach to knowledge. This democratic attitude is seen in the way this research initiative unfolded. The youth involved in this research project came up with the name *The Outside Guide*, and felt this name reflected *their* mandate: 'To create a community resource guide for and by Vancouver Island youth in and out of custody'. We dedicated this research project to two teens: Hunter and Julie. Both had died tragically—Julie by suicide at 19 while attending a drug and alcohol treatment program; Hunter was murdered at the age of 21. Both teens resided in Victoria, British Columbia, and their deaths affected us all.

The Outside Guide provided a unique opportunity for the teens in custody to join in and contribute to their communities and collaborate on a project that encouraged them to organize in peer groups—and it gave these young people the space to voice their concerns about resources (or the lack of them) collectively. It also afforded an opportunity for the youth to learn and work with adult, peer, and mutual support, as well as to master technical design skills that they could continue to utilize upon their release from the custody center. The credit page lists all teens involved in the project and their position. 'Rep' responsibilities included gathering all pertinent youth-friendly information for their community district and then bringing this information to weekly scheduled meetings for group discussion. 'Supporters' were welcome to attend meetings and provided overall input by making suggestions for the group's consideration.

THE OUTSIDE GUIDE BY INSIDE-OUT: a community resource guide for and by Vancouver Island youth in and out of custody was formed in January 2007, as a group of creative minds who felt there was little if any safe, youth friendly programs in their communities. The "resource guide group" provided a weekly forum for teens in custody to not only "rep" their communities while on the "inside," but to come together and collectively research and discuss information that might be of benefit leaving VYCS. Many weeks (and much laughter) later, when info meetings turned into production and design sessions, the guide has kept its mission to provide easily accessible, easy to read and carry, health, recreation, legal and lifestyle information for youths leaving custody. I'd like to thank all the teens and T.B who volunteered their time on this project with the knowledge that future teens leaving VYCS would be given, as Tye so eloquently put it "a helping hand". We hope you find use in this guide/notebook, and that it supports you along your journey. And thank you to those who support and listen to the voice of these young people.

Figure 5.7 Background information for *The Outside Guide*

	CREDIT
GRANT F.	Victoria Rep, Content, Chair #1, Booklet Name
RICCO Z. "Suava"	Port Alberni Rep, Chair #2, Production Manager, File Management
DESMOND W. "Scrunch"	Victoria Rep, Co-Chair, Content Manager, Scrunch's Star Rating ***
SCOTT B. "Teen Wolf"	Illustrator
TYE S. "Scratch"	Cover & Production Designer, InDesign Pre-Press and Layout Illustrator
ZAC V.	Illustrator
COURTNEY D.	Campbell River/Courtenay Rep
JOSH C.	Victoria Rep & Content Creator
JON J., JESSE. G., TONY D.	Nanaimo Reps
WILL E., STAN L.	Cowichan /Duncan Reps
NICK D., KARINE V., BRYCE H.	Photoshop Techs

Supporters: **AMANDA, LYNDA, MELODY, TASHINA**

Figure 5.8 The Outside Guide, credit page

The table of contents guides the reader through an A to Z listing of the following services for Vancouver Island: communities in Victoria, Courtenay/Campbell River, Nanaimo, Cowichan/Duncan, and Port Alberni. 'WWW' lists internet-accessible information.

Table of Contents

VICTORIA	
Counselling	P. 1
ER (Emergency)	P. 6
Employment	P. 7
Food	P. 8
Free	P. 8
Health Services	P. 13
Housing	P. 16
Legal	P. 20
Recreation	P. 24
COURTENAY/CAMPBELL RIVER	P. 31
NANAIMO	P. 34
COWICHAN/DUNCAN	P. 39
PORT ALBERNI	P. 42
WWW	P. 48

Figure 5.9 The Outside Guide, table of contents

A Pathway to Imagine and Build Spaces for Social Advocacy

If we wish to make the case for art as education and therapy, we need to base our claim on the philosophical debates of the experiential outcomes of the art experience and consider the arts as a *contributing* factor to our wellbeing (Cross, 2018, p. 62). The arts help address the *total* minds of its young participants cultivating the full range of a human's potential (Siegesmund, 1998).

As ways of knowing, the arts involve us in complex uses of our intelligences. The arts represent multiple forms of intelligence and multiple ways of knowing, but unlike Piaget's (1970) research suggesting a unilinear development, Gardner (1999) identified differences in the brain for different types of intelligence and the arts as 'tools to develop latent intellectual abilities' (p. 63). He has stated that North American public education generally emphasizes only two of these—linguistic and logical-mathematical—ignoring the other potentials of the mind, and also affirms the need for an education that takes into consideration existential intelligence, or a concern with 'ultimate' issues.

Conclusion

Every generation faces the challenge of preserving and hopefully improving quality of life in our communities. Through arts-based education, critical thinking, and leadership training, young people can develop the skills they need to meet this complex challenge. They should have a voice in shaping their communities and their world. This is not to say that young people don't speak but they are often restricted from speaking in those spheres where public conversation shapes social policy (Giroux, 2003).

Beyond creativity and personal expression, writing and collaborative projects can promote discussions that focus on critical thinking, group discussion processes, conflict resolution, and pro-social networking—personal concerns may become social concerns when shared within a group. The shift in the focus of learning is no longer on the individual alone but the individual *interacting* within a larger socio-cultural context.

When participants have the opportunity to portray their experiences through different art forms, '... it can be a most useful means of engaging them ... and offering them a voice' (Simons and McCormack, 2007, p. 300). Psychologist Jack Kornfield has said that when we bring *respect* to those around us, we open a channel to their own goodness. When youth experience someone who respects and values them, it gives them the ability to admire themselves and others, and I have seen this firsthand when working with incarcerated teens.

The 'reality' is that many detained youth (and some are already parents) have grown up in foster and institutionalized environments, and are subsequently subject to being further traumatized and thus need additional supports after discharge. Experience has taught me that given the support, sense of purpose, and skills needed, every one of us can make choices to improve the quality of our lives regardless of past or present circumstances.

References

Carrell, C. & Laing, J. (1982). *The Special Unit, Barlinnie Prison: Its evolution through its art*. Glasgow: Third Eye.

Chase, S. (2008). *Portraits from the War on Young People: A case study analysis of participants from the Leave Out Violence (LOVE) photojournalism project* (unpublished thesis). Concordia University, QC.

Cross, C. (2002). *Reaching Out: Community art programs as social intervention for 'at risk' youth* (unpublished thesis). University of Victoria, BC.
Cross, C. (2018). *Juvenile Justice and Expressive Arts: Creative disruptions through art programs for and with teens in a correctional institution*. New York: Routledge.
Denshire, S. (1984). *The Shape and Impact of Youth Participation in Health*. Working paper prepared for Study Group on Young People and Health for all by the Year 2000. Geneva, Switzerland: World Health Organization.
Gardner, H. (1999). *Intelligence Reframed: Multiple intelligences for the 21st century*. New York: Basic Books.
Giroux, H.A. (2003). Public pedagogy and the politics of resistance: Notes on a critical theory of educational struggle. *Educational Philosophy & Theory*, 35, 5–16.
Kornfield, J. (2008). *The Wise Heart: A guide to the universal teachings of Buddhist psychology*. New York: Random House.
Lorde, A. (1995). *The Black Unicorn*. New York: Norton.
McLaughlin, M. (2000). *Community Counts: How youth organizations matter for youth development*. Washington, DC: Public Education Network. Retrieved September 25, 2009, from www.publiceducation.org/cgi/bin/download-manager/publications/p.72.asp.
Noam, G.G., Winner, K., Rhein, A., & Molad, B. (1996). The Harvard rally program and the prevention practitioner: Comprehensive, school-based intervention to support resiliency in at-risk adolescents. *Journal of Child and Youth Care Work*, 11, 32–47.
Piaget, J. (1970). *Psychology and Epistemology: Towards a theory of knowledge*. New York: Viking Press.
Siegesmund, R. (1998). Why do we teach art today? *Studies in Art Education*, 39(3), 197–215.
Simons, H. & McCormack, B. (2007). Integrating arts-based inquiry in evaluation methodology: Opportunities and challenges. *Qualitative Inquiry*, 13(2), 292–311.
Smith, R. (1989). Aesthetics in education: Art education a critical necessity. Retrieved June 10, 2004 from www.getty.edu/publications.
Snowman, J. & Biehler, R. (2006). *Psychology Applied to Teaching*. Belmont, CA: Wadsworth Publishing.

Chapter 6

Collaborative Projects

Introduction

How can art programs for incarcerated teens engage participants in effective, collaborative pro-social learning experiences through the arts? Social interaction with adults or peer collaboration enables learning gains that *exceed* what can be attained alone (Snowman & Biehler, 2006). The constructivist approach to learning is based on the premise that cognition is the result of 'mental construction'—in other words, students learn by fitting new information together with what they already know. And in structuring and accomplishing goals, individuals (even in prisons) create novel cognitive developments linked to social life and to their own efforts—this approach is also developmental. With positive peer mentors to identify with, and programming that focuses on helping them develop and see their *strengths* instead of their mistakes, adolescents can begin to consider a better future.

Research Skills

The *Outside Guide* project went beyond the involved teens gathering information and designing a booklet. Incarcerated youth were involved in knowledge creation that allowed them to become active, powerful agents in improving their social group. They were given the opportunity to develop positive connections to self, others, and the larger community—they were empowered to take an active role in shaping their environment.

To summarize, the teens:

1 Researched and discussed the effectiveness (or lack of) social services, health, and recreational organizations in their Vancouver Island communities, and evaluated how these services affected their lives;
2 Identified the overall goals of the research project and how each task was important to the whole;
3 Developed skills to locate, evaluate, and interpret information about those youth-related and community-related resources and brought their personal views on these services to the weekly scheduled meetings where they witnessed how their views were shared, or not, by their peers;
4 Developed an appreciation for and the positive attitude toward regularly scheduled meetings (even scheduling extra meetings to meet publication and printing deadlines), and discussions among their peers, focusing on the tasks at hand;
5 Recognized the interdependence of their peers; their individual roles, and the coordination needed when working within the confines of a correctional institution.

DOI: 10.4324/9781003534082-6

Figure 6.1 Six of *The Outside Guide* researchers
Photograph by Carol Cross.

Figure 6.2 Carol Cross and teens celebrate the completion of *The Outside Guide*
Photograph by Theresa Bennett.

Creative activities foster a sense of *shared* humanity, rather than distancing us from one another. Implementing and engaging in art projects using a range of media to portray lived experiences, alone and with others, may be particularly necessary for humans to survive and flourish in potentially alienating environments (Cynkin & Robinson, 1990). Participation is health enhancing in and of itself and a way of empowering young people, establishing adolescents and adults as partners working together, and recognizing their capabilities. It is also a means of *changing* the mental health system to make it more responsive to young people (Denshire, 1984).

Mental wellbeing needs to be viewed as a vital part of health for the whole population, not just for those who have a mental illness or those at risk of developing mental illness. Collaboration between mental health practitioners, arts education policymakers, and the various other arts and health professionals could determine *new directions* for promoting rehabilitation through the arts. In my experience, I found that self-directed and youth-driven programs fostered a previously absent self-esteem and confidence that will be essential to healthy development when youths return to mainstream society.

The transition of young people from youth and adult correctional facilities—a process termed youth reentry—is one that requires further research to effectively assist this population. Justice-involved children and adolescents face many life challenges, and we need to identify the effectiveness of treatment centers and/or community programs.

Richard Kamler, artist and creator of The Seeing Peace Project, describes art as: "[o]ur one true global language. It knows no nation, it favors no race, and it acknowledges no class. It speaks to our need to reveal, heal, and transform. It transcends our ordinary lives and lets us imagine what is possible" (www.artheals.org/about/power.php, retrieved September 26, 2008).

Youth as Collaborators and Curriculum Builders

Whether we find ourselves working in a correctional institution or in the community sphere, whether as counselors, art program coordinators or facilitators, if we strive to design programs that improve society and the ways in which young people think, then the young people for whom we design our programs need to be directly involved. With this in mind, the *Peer-Support Workbook* in the second part of this book is a culmination of creative writing and art exercises. Instead of being held down by personal trauma and violence, participants took ownership and gained the experience of 'authorship'.

A progressive curriculum, structured in nine units, each unit features a sequence of lessons organized with a theme and concludes with a writing and/or art exercise. It is a useful resource for professionals working with youth identified as having delinquent or at-risk tendencies.

References

Cynkin, S. & Robinson, A.M. (1990). *Occupational Therapy and Activities Health: Toward health through activities*. Boston, MA: Little, Brown.

Denshire, S. (1984). *The Shape and Impact of Youth Participation in Health*. Working paper prepared for Study Group on Young People and Health for all by the Year 2000. Geneva, Switzerland: World Health Organization.

Snowman, H., & Biehler, R. (2006). *Psychology Applied to Teaching*. Belmont, CA: Wadsworth Publishing.

Postscript – Moving Forward

Reverend Jesse L. Jackson, Sr. (2000) speaks to the importance of our collective involvement in reclaiming our youth: 'and where there is hope there is life, where there is life there is possibility, and where there is possibility change can occur.'

We need to broaden our definition of the term 'art' and the way we approach it, value it, and educate others with and through it, ensuring we take into consideration socio-economic and language differences, intergenerational trauma, as well as challenge oft held stereotypes. We also need to recognize that witnessing violence and other adverse childhood experiences can lead to ongoing health problems, resulting in emotional and physical ailments.

Throughout the Western world, we continue to hear about the increase in youth violence, adolescent gangs, and a decrease in funding for youth employment and alternative education initiatives. As we seek solutions to these problems, we need to build partnerships and develop inter-organizational relationships.

Community regeneration is accomplished by fostering innovative partnerships between art and social service agencies; creating safe havens for 'at-risk' and 'high risk' youth and families particularly in unsafe neighborhoods; strengthening participants' inner resources (self-esteem, self-awareness, identity, confidence, and tolerance for others); and integrating multiple areas of participants' lives (home, school, health, etc.). We need to think outside mainstream educational systems and build programs designed to serve as catalysts for the creative process—initiatives that provide youth with a venue for sharing and setting goals for their futures.

If we are committed to a vision of creativity as a catalyst for change, we need to unite so that our voices will be more powerful. Parents, youths, and community members need to be the decision-makers and have input, to interact and learn from one another. I hope we continue to see an increasing number of organizations building sustainable and consistent programming for disadvantaged children, youth, and families while sharing their knowledge and resources with others.

I have witnessed 'at-risk' youth develop into young men and women making positive changes in their lives—attending college and university, and making decisions that have ultimately been instrumental to improving their attitudes about themselves and their future. Through encouragement and support, they see that they do have a choice. This has strengthened my belief that community programs can play a role in improving the odds for teens in need. They provide avenues through which we can encourage and nurture while instilling needed life skills and benefiting at-risk youth—but the hands reaching out to help them must be ours.

Successful community development programs are adapted, not replicated, from other programs. The most effective are developed in response to the specific needs and resources of a community. We need to acknowledge and support the growing number of young individuals who are becoming social activists in their work by setting up programs in public places that result in benefits for everyone involved.

To be a socially engaged community artist is to be committed to art as social activism—a hybrid of political activism and community organizing. The goal as a social intervention is for everyone to be empowered through the creative process, to acquire a voice, visibility, and an awareness that we are all part of a whole. The aim is to make a contribution, and hopefully, a lasting impact on the lives of those involved. Nothing is impossible when we support those around us. Empathy is not appropriation of another's experience, but an appropriate *connection* with others. Implementing and engaging in creative arts-based projects, using a range of media to portray lived experiences, alone and with others, may be particularly necessary for humans to survive and flourish in potentially alienating environments. And this can foster a community that is both broad and deep, where people of radically different backgrounds can find common ground by sharing.

Finally, I have been greatly influenced by what young people have had to say, and it is important for me to acknowledge them for their impact on my research, this project, and on my own personal growth. Participants teach us that being involved in the arts is not merely a pastime, but an opportunity to rise above our circumstances and express the best part of us. And that art instruction in a variety of art disciplines and workshops also offers a refuge from the prison environment. I believe in the power of the arts as an effective instrument for healing, community integration, and institutional and social change. Justice-involved children and teens can build transferable life skills, leading them to seek out additional opportunities in higher education, trades, or rehabilitative programs. It can offer a refuge from the restrictive prison environment and locked cell door—to humanize life otherwise lacking in color, creativity, and joy. Community intervention pays more attention to promoting a more humane deterrent to divert those at risk of entering the criminal justice system.

Though written in 1934, 90 years ago, John Dewey's words couldn't seem more contemporary:

> Out of the urgency we are now experiencing, caused by the greed of those without imagination who have been allowed to rule for too long, will come the search for language and images rich and complex enough to represent the economic and spiritual path many are now [hoping to] experience ...

Note: Portions of this book have appeared in the following publication: *Juvenile Justice and Expressive Arts: Creative Disruptions through Art Programs for and with Teens in a Correctional Institution.*

Acknowledgements

This project would not have been possible without the many individuals who supported me; individuals who were committed to my projects over the years, volunteering their time and creative talents. Once again, thank you to Pat R. who accepted my invitation to provide his insights. Rafael F. for his insights as a former correctional officer, and Tye S. for a heart-warming letter—words that, again, have made the writing of this publication all the more meaningful.

Dedication

This project is dedicated to those young writers and artists whose lives have touched mine *and* to those who support and listen to the voice of these young people.

Reference

Jackson, Sr., J.L. (2000). Foreword. In W. Ayers, R. Ayers, & B. Dohm (Eds.) *Resisting Zero Tolerance*. New York: The New Press.

Appendices

Appendix A

A Reflective Letter by Patrick (Pat) R.

When I was first asked by Carol to contribute to a paper exploring the importance of art in correctional institutions my initial reaction was to pass on the opportunity. Writing is what I did while I was in prison, so now that I am not, I shy away from it. At least that's my excuse. Writing well is very difficult, and after spending 18 years in custody, I'm experiencing quite a few difficulties reintegrating back to society, so I really didn't need another one to add to my woes. That's another excuse. The truth is, my involvement with *Out of Bounds* magazine, a quarterly publication produced by the prisoners at William Head Institution, a Federal penitentiary just outside of Victoria, British Columbia, helped me survive a long prison sentence, helped me become a better person, and, I hope, helped prisoners, prison staff, and the public gain insight into the carceral experience. So I actually owe a lot to the people who promote the arts within correctional institutions.

As far as I can ascertain from the research I did for an article on the history of the magazine, *Out of Bounds* began publication on September 4, 1980. The premiere issue was called *Out of Bounds: William Head Institution Newsletter*. Using a typical newsletter format, the founding felons incorporated an atypical logo: a medieval woodcut depicting what I can only construe to be the town fool thumbing his nose at society—very apropos I might say. That inaugural issue quoted Oscar Wilde from his "The Ballad of Reading Gaol" on its front page:

> The vilest deeds like poison weeds,
> Bloom well in prison air;
> It is only what is good in man
> That wastes and withers there.

Although it isn't stated explicitly in any subsequent issues, it appears the publication's genesis was inspired by the University of Victoria's Department of Education's post-secondary degree program that was taking place at William Head at the time. The same university program generated the inspiration that led to the formation of a prison theatre society in 1981. Now named WHoS (William Head on Stage), it continues to provide quality theatre for prisoners and the paying public to this day. My involvement with *Out of Bounds* began in 1993 when I arrived at William Head, after transferring from Mission Institution, and continued until my release to Victoria on day parole in 2002.

My involvement with writing had begun several years earlier when a psychologist at the Regional Health Centre, a special needs prison that provides extensive programs for violent offenders, suggested that I take up writing to better understand and express my emotions, something I always had trouble doing and subsequently often got me in trouble. So I began writing poetry, then short stories, then non-fiction articles. Writing not only helped me understand and express my emotions, but more importantly, it helped me understand some of the complicated social issues that culminated in me taking another man's life. Writing helped make my lengthy stay in prison a productive one. Writing is an important educational experience, a process that inevitably leads to the development of character and mental powers.

My involvement with *Out of Bounds* extended well beyond simply writing. For close to 10 years I was the editor and publisher of the magazine as well. The educational experience that comes from publishing a prison magazine is truly unique and indescribably valuable. It is far beyond the scope of this particular article to discuss the means and ends of prison pedagogy. It's difficult enough trying to come up with a working definition of education within the custodial milieu. If education involves learning, when you're sentenced to do a semester in the 'school of hard knocks' you'll learn a difficult lesson every day if you're not careful. The real purpose of education in general has been variously described as individual empowerment, personal development, formal instruction, enlightenment, guidance and discipline. I prefer to simply call it growth, qualified by the designations: spiritual and mental. In my opinion, educational instruction in prison deserves a dual purpose: it enables an inmate to overcome deficiencies such as being illiterate, under-educated and/or under-qualified for trade training; and it serves to prepare an inmate to better comprehend, and thus benefit from, the rehabilitative programs that he or she will be required to participate in. In contrast, the pattern of education a prisoner-initiated enterprise can provide extends well beyond the 'correctional' purposes just mentioned.

The tutelage encountered while participating in a prisoner-initiated enterprise such as *Out of Bounds* speaks more to the psychological and intellectual well-being of the participants during their incarceration, as opposed to the illusive spectre of rehabilitation that correctional programs cater to. One peculiarity of the 'medical model' of corrections, the model most in use today, presupposes that criminals are inflicted with some sort of social ill, and a stint in the penitentiary will somehow (with the aid of countless programs, constant badgering, and a pinch of punishment) miraculously cure this ill so the 'rehabilitated' offender can return to society as a law-abiding citizen. Unfortunately, part of this 'cure' involves being separated from and scapegoated by society; it involves being labeled, dehumanized and degraded; it involves the loss of rights, self-respect and self-determination; but most importantly, it involves the loss of community. I believe that most crime comes about when the perpetrator loses touch with the essence of community and the commonweal essential to its survival.

One of the most important qualities of community that I turned my back on when I entered a criminal lifestyle was the practice of joining together as a group to accomplish common goals for the good of the whole community. Unfortunately, my involvement in crime resulted in me becoming extremely self-centered and selfish, showing little concern for the well-being of others. In contrast, my involvement with *Out of Bounds* helped alleviate quite a bit of that egoistic attitude and behavior. Participating in inmate-initiated endeavors contrasts markedly with taking correctional programs. Inmate-initiated endeavors are voluntary as opposed to mandatory; they concentrate on personal development as opposed to character 'correction'; they encourage excellence as opposed to punishing error; they promote creativity as opposed to enforcing discipline; and most importantly, because inmate-initiated endeavors impart a strong sense of ownership to their participants, positive feelings of self-esteem and self-determination often result, a benefit that not only allows for immediate learning but also encourages further exploration, creating an upward-spiraling process of mental and spiritual growth.

There are several complementary 'rehabilitative' features arising from inmate-initiated endeavors as well. I suppose that's why prison administrators inevitably allow (sometimes even encourage) their existence. Specifically, with a project whose primary purpose is communication, the process of enhancing one's ability to express his or her accomplishment, disappointments, complaints and concerns in an objective, pro-social manner is at once educational and rehabilitative. Through this process one can gain experiential knowledge and a methodology of understanding that assists them in every-day interaction with both institutional staff and fellow inmates. Experiential learning is an important aspect of any endeavor. We learn best by doing. Didactic programs offered by correctional institutions often fail miserably because they involve less than impartial instructors (prison personnel) lecturing less than enthusiastic participants (coerced inmates) with a premise that is a controversial as it is demeaning (you're defective, we can fix you). Rehabilitation is more effectively realized when the person who is being rehabilitated perceives that he or she has a stake in that process. With inmate-initiated projects that perception is a self-evident outcome. The sense of ownership these endeavors impart upon their participants coalesces with the resultant feelings of self-determination and together they fuel further learning, dignity and decorum.

Marshall McLuhan, one of Canada's leading scholars (recently deceased) who was routinely called a media guru and the oracle of the electric age, turned the world of communications on its head when he stated that 'the medium is the message'. He postulated that the form of a particular medium is more important than the content. I tend to disagree. I believe that the message a prison publication imparts is a medium through which personal growth can be realized for all of those who grace its pages, read its message, or are involved in its production. I witnessed considerable growth in the attitudes and abilities of many contributors to *Out of Bounds*. Thankfully, my involvement in that literary endeavor initiated quite a bit of positive growth of my own. This growth, or reform, or what correctional institutions are wont to call rehabilitation, is the cumulative effect of several alterations in attributes and opportunities. Without doubt, the singular most significant altered attribute would have to be the higher self-esteem and its concomitant increase in feelings of self-worth that one experiences from having his or her writing or art published. And perhaps the most ostensive opportunity a prison publication provides is as a venue for disseminating discontent, an experience which can actually alleviate some of the frustrations that prisoners often accumulate from not having a voice. These frustrations, if they are not expressed in an appropriate manner, can lead to destructive thoughts and aberrant behavior. Ideally, a message is the means to an end. So, stated differently, the message is the medium. More specifically, the message in a prison publication is the medium for change. This change can encompass thoughts, feelings, attitudes and behaviors; but more importantly, it heralds enlightenment. Education is the ultimate end. Producing a prison publication is an educational experience bar none.

The message in *Inside-Out*, a publication I'm currently involved with that is by and for youth in custody, emanates from the writing and art published in the magazine.

Although there can be a different statement expressed in each individual submission, the overall representation is one of contrite hope and realization. By being honest and open and willing to share their thoughts and feelings with their readers in an authentic manner, some of the misconceptions that surround incarceration and the incarcerated can be dispelled. And by enunciating one's own shortcomings, a person in custody can come to the important realization that he or she can 'fix' themselves—that they can 'become' rehabilitated a lot easier and more effectively than 'be' rehabilitated. We learn that we need to examine and criticize the underlying aberrant attitudes and beliefs that led to our criminal activity with as much rigor and enthusiasm as we expend criticizing the criminal justice system. But in doing so we needn't let that system off completely either. Society has to bear some complicity in our social 'illness' and learn to prevent that illness rather than try to punish it into remission.

The message in *Inside-Out* is one of emancipation. Writing (as well as producing other art forms) is a liberating sentiment. The opportunity to voice one's concerns and opinions in a prison publication, combined with the educational experience that comes from learning how to write effectively, in an objective manner, speaks to the psychological and intellectual well-being touched upon earlier in this article. If prisoners believe that they can make positive changes, their incarceration becomes less troublesome in both scope and duration.

If people in custody can learn to accomplish things for the common good of their little microcosm of society, a microcosm replete with an abundance of hate, anger, violence and selfishness, then in a sense they are liberating themselves from those otherwise negative constraints. If *Inside-Out* can nurture an honest (often sorely lacking) sense of altruism in its participants, then it becomes much more than just an inmate-initiated educational aid and a rehabilitative tool cherished by the institution's administration, it becomes a character-building message, the medium for social change.

During my years with *Out of Bounds*, it always encouraged me when I observed, from issue to issue (sometimes from year to year), the positive growth in both ability and attitude of my fellow prison writers and artists. I took pride in assuming that in some small way the magazine helped facilitate that growth. The process of taking a small piece of crumpled paper shyly submitted by a so-called hardened criminal, knowing that he has agonized relentlessly over the writing of that article or poem (in some cases taken a heart-felt risk due to its content), then filtering that submission through the regimen of editing, layout, printing and binding, resulting in what many people believe is one of North American's best prison publications, has its own rewards. For me the reward lies in the look of apprehension, then pride, that emanates from the fellow who made the submission when I hand him his copy of the finished product and he sees his work in print.

In closing, I want to leave you with another quote by Oscar Wilde, the illustrious author-cum-convict:

> I need not remind you that mere expression is to an artist the supreme and only mode of life. It is by utterance we live. Of the many, many things for which I have to thank the Governor there is none for which I am more grateful than for his permission to write fully and at as great length as I desire.
>
> (Patrick R., 2005, reprinted in its entirety with permission, 2024).

Appendix B

A Reflective Letter by Rafael Fuentes

As the youths' counselor, Carol also implemented arts programs that had a positive impact on the youth at the correctional facility. The youth were encouraged to be creative and thoughtful. The *Inside-Out Magazine* allowed the youth to articulate peer support and self-reflection. Also, I remember the games room (on four units) being transformed with Carol's mural program; decorating bare walls. There were many inspiring Indigenous and non-Indigenous images like the two hands together for gratitude, and it made the walls colorful.

The teens that committed to the arts program were always excited to go, and they came back to their units in good spirits. Carol Cross' art programs, and *Inside-Out Magazine*, for teens at the custody center, left a positive, lasting impression on the youth.

Thank you, Carol.
Rafael Fuentes
Youth Correctional Officer (1997–2013),
Victoria Youth Custody Center (VYCC)
(Rafael Fuentes, printed in its entirety with permission, 2022).

Appendix C

A Reflective Letter by Tye S.

My name is Tye S. I have been in and out of the youth correction centers since July 18th, 2005. My view on everyday life was obscenely destructive and I was considered hopeless. In February of 2007, I was transferred from the Burnaby Youth Custody Centre to the Victoria branch, in hope of receiving help I couldn't get previous from my move. This new move opened up a new and powerful relationship with a woman named Carol Cross that has changed parts of my life for the better, and has set me on a new path. In working with Carol, I have learned many new things which involve graphic design on a new and undoubtedly earned computer. Involvement with self-publishing magazines called '*Inside-Out*', and a forgotten passion to write all the feelings inside of me out on to paper to share with anyone interested. Another thing that we accomplished as a team was *The Outside Guide* by Inside-Out, a resource guide for the sole purpose to help teens in need.

I will never forget all of the hard work and passion that Carol put into helping the teens. This woman has convinced me, and helped me achieve my new goal in going to college which never occurred to me a possible feat. I owe much to Carol Cross and will miss her lots. Hopefully, this is of help and gets through.

(Tye S., March 30, 2008)

Part II

PEER-SUPPORT WORKBOOK

Words from the Inside-Out

Compiled by Carol Cross, PhD

This workbook has depended on the wisdom of young writers to discuss topics central to their lives and adheres to strong confidentiality restrictions.

Contents

Unit 1	Introduction: Tapping into Creativity	80
Unit 2	Self-image	83
Unit 3	Life	89
Unit 4	Feelings	92
Unit 5	Here to There	97
Unit 6	Drugs and Violence	106
Unit 7	Love and Loss	114
Unit 8	Relationships	119
Unit 9	Choice and Having Your Say	125

Figures

U1.1 Self-portrait, ink pen drawing, by I.O. 80
U2.1 Photograph, Entering the Victoria Youth Custody Centre 83
U3.1 Photograph, VYCC, Unit 2, Secure Custody, basketball players 89
U5.1 *Inside-Out Magazine, A Retrospective*, cover and credits 97
U5.2 Victoria Youth Custody Centre (VYCC), "Horror-scopes" 103
U5.3 Victoria Youth Custody Centre (VYCC), C.D., 'Tupac' drawing and wood burning on panel 104
U6.1 Photograph, Victoria Youth Custody Centre (VYCC), six of *The Outside Guide* researchers 106
U7.1 Drawing on wood with burning, feathers, and acrylic paint, by W.E. 114
U7.2 Wooden chest, by T. 115
U7.3 Drawing, wood burning on panel, by T. 116
U7.4 North Coast Wolf, acrylic on paper, by Anon 117
U8.1 Pencil on paper, by A.M. 119
U8.2 "Thunderbird and Salmon," acrylic on paper, by T. 121
U9.1 Mural, by Tashina A. and Carol Cross (40′ × 48′) 125
U9.2 Mural, "Love, Peace & Harmony," by Jesse T., Kyle P., Tony D., Carol Cross, Bryce H. (15′ × 8′) 130
U9.3 Mural, Pacific Mid Coast, Kneeling human releasing a hummingbird (53′ × 39′) by Alex M., Carol Cross, Chris J., Cody J., David C. 133

Introduction

Tapping into Creativity

To be alive at all involves some risk.

Figure U1.1 Self-portrait, ink pen drawing, by I.O.

Life Is a Journey

We all get to make, storing up memories as a keepsake. Hold on to the good times and learn from the sad; sometimes it's the little things that are the best things you have had. Remember your loved ones, they are the most important part, and share with one another straight from the heart. Don't ever regret it as long as you live; you shall get from each other as long as you give.

A Good Life

What is a good life? Many people have thoughts on what a good life is, and what a good life is not. When I think of a good life, I think of a happy place without stress and strife. I think of people helping each other as if they were your own brother, child or mother. I think of the rich giving to the poor, giving everyone the chance to spread their wings and soar. If we could only tell how we all have a special purpose, some will tell but some will never surface. We're given these talents so we can work as a team. They are made to form a balance, just like stitching a seam.

So as you can tell we all play a role, it's like that saying 'my glass isn't half empty but half full.' It's hard to live a good life when people don't work together. Some days you might feel happy, but this feeling won't last forever. So these are my thoughts on living a good life ... ***what are yours?***

Writing / Art Exercise

My life would be different if I ... (finish the sentence)

Tapping into creativity: this workbook is your personal ongoing project.

Find an image that best typifies how you are feeling. This can be a drawing or a magazine clipping. Write about it: the subject matter, why you chose it.

Self-research: consider yourself—your life before, your life now, your future, recurring issues, concerns, questions, situations that you like or dislike, your beliefs. Record your thoughts in drawings, journal writing, or a poem.

Use colors, patterns, drawings, or words to describe yourself.

Unit 2

Self-image

Figure U2.1 Photograph, Entering the Victoria Youth Custody Centre

Photograph by Carol Cross.

Shattered Dreams

A wasted youth and shattered dreams, life is never what it seems.

Time for a change is drawing near, but don't be afraid, you've nothing to fear. Death and violence behind a locked door, sands of the hourglass fall forever more.

Look in the mirror, what do you see? Anger and hatred staring back at me. The eyes are dead with a phony smile, look closer my friend you will see denial. A lonely existence in a cell I call home; no friends or family, I'm all alone.

Some turn to violence, others turn to dope, neither is wrong it's just how we cope. This is the reality that I face each day, and as the night wears on I dream away. Sooner or later from this dream I'll awake, another day of my life the system will take. The shadow of a man, from a boy I once knew, this isn't bullshit, every word is true. After my death is when I'll be free, it'll be much too late, no chance to be me.

Hidden

I have seen things that many others haven't. I have done things many others won't do. I have a knowledge of the streets and war, but is this what I really want? My life is like a roller coaster, and I can't seem to get off.

My heartaches and my heart closes, but still I wish for more.

You look at me and laugh. I look at you and weep. My life could be so much more, but I keep on choosing the wrong paths. I am part of the world that exists behind brick walls.

Me

Swirl of color, fabric of silk, breakfast as simple as cornflakes and milk. Occult fascinates and horror chills, I'm just a teenager finding some thrills.

Beaches of white, oceans of blue, the love of my life and it's true. Nature and music entwine as one, homework and papers and books done. Friends misunderstand is what I can't stand. Why don't they take me as I am? I rebel but without a cause to change all within me that is flawed.

Understand me, it is not very hard, emotions play a very big part. Thoughts of mine fly the colors in time, sing songs of harmony that fall in rhyme. Try to understand me is all I ask, try to understand me and this too shall pass.

Inside (Anger)

It's my attitude that's making me bust shit. Never in a million years would I have dreamed so many people like me share the same thoughts; the same exact beliefs. It's like an army marching in back of me.

So much anger just sprays and sprays. I don't give a shit about what you think of me, just please let me be. Honest to god I just try to keep to myself, but when the rest of the world is out to get me, there is nothing left to do except to fight back with words first. Ask them ... why are you doing this? Why are you treating me this way? I never did anything to you. Tell them to think before they act. Before you hit someone, picture them as your little brother or sister. Could you do this to them? Or picture your mother or father... but maybe they're a person who just plain doesn't care.

My advice is if you have a lot of anger let it out in different ways. Ways that won't hurt you or anybody else. Talk to someone who will listen, someone who cares. It helps ... it helps a lot! It helps to sort out your mixed emotions. It helps you find the true you hiding behind all your anger and pain. It helps you get out and interact with other people. It helped me sort out 70% of my anger; but the remainder 30% of my pain is too deep to deal with so I try to ignore it. Sometimes it just builds up past the point and I unleash all of my anger and hatred within me. I am still the lone wolf. I like to be alone, away from everyday life and all of the noise that goes with it. One day I'll have the courage to knock over the tower of pain, anger, and confusion. Here's a little more advice: live life one day at a time; keep true to yourself. Believe in yourself and remember that anything is possible.

Believe in what makes you feel good. Believe in what makes you happy. Believe in the dreams you've always wanted to come true and give them every chance to. No one knows the ultimate meaning of life, but for those who believe in their dreams and in their self; life is a precious gift in which anything is possible. Most people believe you only have one life to live so they try to live it to its fullest, but I still live life one day at a time.

The Real True Me

The smile that I wear, not many see through it. Does anyone know the things I hide? Through my laughter and smiles, my happy eyes, does anyone know how I feel inside?

There's not yet anybody close enough for me to confide. Does anyone bother to think before they judge? They see my exterior, they hate before they know. I don't think at any time the real true me I show.

Does anyone know how much I just want to scream? Does anyone care to wonder what nightmares haunt my dreams? Everyday I hear snide remarks; catch cold glares thrown my way. Does anybody know how much I really have to say? Do you ever wonder why I laugh and smile so? Maybe it's because I don't want to remember the things I know. Maybe it's because I'm struggling to not let my sadness show. You think I'm only attention seeking when I call myself down.

Did you honestly believe my smile wasn't masking a frown? Don't tell me that I'm pretty, it's this I can't endure, because none of you could possibly see what I see in the mirror. I wish somebody knew how much I honestly feel fear. And I wish somebody knew how many are my hidden tears.

If only one person could see into the dark of my sad past; I would highly doubt they would be so quick to judge so fast. I wish somebody would tell me how long this pain will last. This smile that I wear is drowning out the cries, choking on the lies, showing hope that's died.

You don't know me the way you think you do. You can't see the thoughts up in my head. You can't count the countless tears I've shed. If you could only see my bruised and broken soul, how inside I'm sad and cold, would you still look at me with scorn?

Doesn't anybody know how sometimes I wish I wasn't born? How many times I'm smiling but still feeling so forlorn? Doesn't anybody see how many times my heart's been torn?

Please don't be fooled by this smile that I wear, there's so much hiding there.

Use this space to write about what creative talents you'd like to pursue.

What are you passionate about?

Self-image: Describe the quality about yourself that you MOST LIKE. It can be a physical characteristic or an aspect of your personality. Choose five things that you like about yourself.

1.

2.

3.

4.

5.

What do you think others think of you? Would they be wrong or right?

What would you change, if anything, about yourself?

Pick a friend, relative, or an acquaintance who is VERY DIFFERENT from you. An example is if you are a soft-spoken person, pick someone who is more aggressive. Write about him or her. Would you want to be like that person? If yes, why? If no, then why not?

Use this blank page to draw your self-image.

Unit 3

Life

Bitterness imprisons life; love and forgiveness release it.

Figure U3.1 Photograph, VYCC, Unit 2, Secure Custody, basketball players

Photograph by Carol Cross.

Life

I want to be the best and make it.

I never want to be a known as a flunk or a fake. I got to keep on going knowing my birth was no mistake. Real is the way to be, no other way to live. I know it's up to me to make it that way.

Keep your mind straight it is all up to you. A good-hearted soul will help you stay true, and with a pure heart I can make it come true, but don't ever forget … it's all up to you.

I Am a Survivor

Every day is a struggle for some, for some it's not. Some have a perfect grasp on the world, and some are just lost. Lost in the world of delightful lies, the drug wars, and family ties. It is hard to get out, to keep your nose clean, to turn away from peer pressure, to be heard, and to be seen.

Every day consists of the choices you make, so keep your head up and turn away from the fake. I once was lost, caught up in the drugs and crime. The choices I made got me doing time. I can't count how many times I've been in here. I can't count my endless tears, but life goes on. I tell myself to keep my head held high. I'm a strong-willed warrior; I know I will survive.

Comfort Zone

My cell is as cold as ice. The more things I get to put in there, the more it feels like home. My comfort sets in as I get used to it, but when will I truly get used to it?

Two years … and I feel there is something missing. I think and think and realize it's my freedom. I sit in this world of destruction, thinking of how I could turn out this way. I act and sound like one that could never love another, but this is not true.

For once, I let my barriers down. I am not guarded by my front anymore and it hurts. I am still one that people would look at in disgust for my crimes aren't minor, and these people that are gone can never return.

Growing Pains

The pain of sorrow, the pain to fight, the pain of tomorrow, the pain to see the light, the pain is within, the pain is so strong, the pain will begin, the pain is so long.

The pain in everything, the pain in us all, the pain in the living, the pain grows tall. The pain in each other, the pain in our lives, the pain in a brother, the pain in our wives, the pain is growing, the pain of fate, the pain is growing, and this pain is my trait.

Reality on the 'Inside'

At night, I sit by my window and daydream about the real world. I'm still in reality here, but it's different. I'm restricted of anything and everything. I can't get a job like I used to be able to. I have to ask to clear my plate of food. If one piece of cutlery is not returned after a meal, we all get our rooms ripped apart, strip-searched and we're locked until it is found.

Some days, I feel like an animal locked in a cage. I find myself gazing at the ceiling and not even knowing what I'm feeling. Pain, ashamed, sadness, anger, loneliness! I don't know, it's all bundled up and it hurts deep inside of my soul. I know every day my criminal past has left an emotional scar that will forever last. Now that I have freed myself from all my dirty deeds, and as I sit and pray to god on my own two knees, I ask the lord for peace. I also ask the lord to help us all, because we all must conquer our own brick wall. And even though I am in lockdown, in my heart I know I am free.

Having Hope

To live and let live, to forgive and forget, there are things in life you'll never regret. Life can be cruel in so many ways, just do better things and have greater days.

Don't think in the past but look ahead, if we live in denial, we end up dead. Think of the future, could be clearer and bright, if I do know anything, I'll put up that fight. That fight to be free, a fight to be strong, I want to just live a good life so nothing will go wrong.

Some of the common themes in this unit are: emotional hurt, making wrong choices, and searching for a sense of belonging.

Writing Exercise

How does YOUR personal history inform your life?

Who can you turn to for emotional support: a friend, family, relative, elder, or ...?

Unit 4

Feelings

Anger

To me anger is mental, verbal abuse. Maybe something could have happened to someone in their past life to get someone full of hate and rage. It's crazy about all the violence that happens with anger. How when people are mad they will take their anger out on whatever comes in their way. Some people are under the influence of drugs and alcohol and don't really remember what they had done wrong. There are so many different ways that people deal with their anger.

Sometimes it may get out of hand; people have their own strategy of how they deal with anger. Nowadays, all we see is anger. People are getting murdered; getting stabbed; people overdosing because they are angry and mad at the world.

For myself, I have so much anger and hate but if I let it build up in me that is when little things happen that can piss me off, and all of that anger comes out and I am rude, and I don't really care about what happens next.

Things like this writing exercise on anger is what people need to change their lives. Violence isn't the answer. Anger is one of the strongest emotions. Never let anger control you. Make a change in yourself. Be yourself, not someone that you are not. No matter what, you might still have anger inside of you, but try to express your anger in other ways. Every day I think of new ways to try and control my anger. You can too. It takes one step at a time.

Anger is an emotion. The writer moved beyond reflecting on the causes and consequences of anger to a position of taking personal responsibility for controlling her emotions. She outlines her strategy of finding a pro-social outlet like writing, and encourages the reader to do so as well. Her story was written in response to my question to the group: 'What does anger feel or look like to you?'

Describe what anger feels or looks like to you.

Dealing with Anger

Remember that anger is a natural emotion

You have the right to feel angry when you are hurt, exploited, ignored, manipulated, frustrated, cheated, or rejected. But anger does not have to lead to violence. You can choose to deal with your anger constructively.

Acknowledge that you are angry

As soon as you possibly can, tell the person(s) you are angry at why you are angry. If that is not possible, at least speak to someone.

Sometimes anger is so extreme that we feel out of control. Be aware of some normal physical signs of anger, such as jitters, a racing heart, irregular breathing, stammering, and clenched fists.

You may need to take certain steps before you are ready to express your anger without violence. What are some steps that you can take? Most people would advise counting to ten ... does that work? Go for a walk? Punch a pillow? And if not, why?

As soon as you are able to, go back and talk about why you are angry.

Here are some examples of how you could approach someone who has made you angry:

- 'I am angry because you called me stupid. I deserve to be treated with respect.'
- 'I am angry because you ignore me when I am talking to you. I would appreciate your stopping to listen to what I have to say.'

What has worked in the past for you? What has not worked?

Thoughts ... Dealt with Feelings

The feelings and thoughts mixed in your head and it's hard to see a person sleeping with no bed. Every morning he goes to the soup kitchen just to be fed. People have problems the rich man said. You can be a millionaire and unhappy. You could be poor but happy it's your choice. You must decide.

A Simple Smile, a Scream Inside

There is so much no one knows about the way I feel inside. My thoughts and all my needs, maybe it's that they don't look or the fact I don't show. Either way there are things inside that no one seems to know.

I want to show the world, I want everyone to see all of the thoughts and ideas that flow inside of me.

A simple smile is what you see, but I am not content or the person I seem to be. There's a different person inside that I can't seem to show. But maybe if you took the time that person you could know.

Hollow

I've walked down this hall before into empty rooms through open doors. Each room as empty as the feelings I hold inside; all of this kills my pride. Inside my mind a place I like to hide, inside my brain another kind of pain, need some meds going insane, this shit's the same, like every day.

Why do kids gotta go through so much pain these days? It's got to the point where you have to watch what you say. Passion for your dreams is slowly slipping away. I'm told that maybe this is all just a phase, but what if it's not? I never thought I would be sitting in jail, on welfare, no money for my bail.

There's so much pain. Life is kind of like a game. Play it right, choose your fights, and you might be on your way, but I have so many friends who wish their life would come to an end. Can't say I haven't been there. Hell, I've been down that road, but that's not where I want to be. I thought I knew what I wanted, and did it until it was done.

A dream is what you want to do, but still haven't pursued. What are yours?

____

____

____

____

____

____

Alone (Foster Care)

Sitting alone in the silence, left with only thoughts of violence. Not long ago I threw a fit simply wishing I had someone to hit. They're always trying to send me away, send me away to another place to stay. Now farther than ever before, I never know what they have in store. All I do is sit and wait, falling deeper within this depressed state. Why can't they just leave me alone? All I want is to be on my own. If they don't want me to roam, why won't they find me a home?

I walk this path alone. My thoughts and feelings are my companions. Everyone pushes me away, as if to say, we do not want you.

Loneliness kicks in and I begin to cry. I wonder to myself about all the things I could do ... and all the decisions I have to make.

My Friend, Pain

What do I do when I'm full of hurt and pain? Cause I can't keep freaking out and going totally insane. I feel that pain is going to get me anyway. I can't keep it out. I try to ignore as if it never exists.

When I bow down and cry, it keeps coming around just to say hi. He's been like a buddy through every day that I live. He continues to come, no matter how much he's already give. We're too close, I can't just ask him to go away, because even when I do, he doesn't care about what I say. Two heads are better than one, so can you help me out because I need to know what else my life is about?

Use this space for self-reflection.

In Unit Four, teens talk about strong feelings, like personal pain and stress.

Stress is a part of life, and we all experience stress on a daily basis. But sometime stress can become overwhelming like when you have to make a big decision.

Writing Exercise

What are some positive things you can think of that can help handle stress?

Make a list of things that give you pleasure. Then choose one and try to describe it in detail.

Here to There

Figure U5.1 Inside-Out Magazine, A Retrospective, cover and credits

Never compare yourself with anyone else, just be yourself and remember, just because someone else can't do it, or chose not to do it, doesn't mean you can't!

Here to There

It's hard to get from here to there if you never get out of bed. You lie a lot to fool your friends, but you fooled yourself instead. It's harder to get from here to there, if you set your goals too high, then nothing ever works out right, and then too soon you no longer try. The hardest way to get from here to there is when all you ever do is count the years and miles to go.

So how do you get from here to there? Well, you first must believe you can. Let no one tell you differently. It's your life, and it's in your hands. Then turn your dreams into your goals and see what you need to satisfy the requirements. The why, the where, and how, at first you're overwhelmed. There is so much you don't know, but keep your faith, be strong and sure, for you do have a way to go.

Take careful steps and do them right, take pride in each thing done. Don't look too far ahead of yourself, just that next step yet to come. Before you know it, you'll be there; your dream will then be real. And you'll be standing where I am now, telling others how good it feels. You'll tell them not to quit on themselves, to have faith though it's hard to hear, so they will know it can be done and they too can get from here to there.

Time for Change

Sick and tired of being hurt from the decisions I foolishly make. Of seeking love and the happiness of being wanted, but lost is how I really feel, confused and wounded, and now my future at stake. My past and those evil and nasty decisions will always haunt me.

Always seeking the next chance to run. And the next shelter in which I can hide. This lifestyle has run out of mind games and fun. I feel as though I'm on a roller coaster and it's the end of the ride. Wanting to find a place where I truly belong. Labeled as an outcast, always out of place; it's time to change myself.

Sitting alone on top of a tainted bridge, crawling closer to death every day by a smidge, wishing I couldn't feel, so my pain within would go away or heal. I grew up quickly on my own, although I never felt this empty or alone. I cry my pain like pouring blood, day after day, hoping someone would hear what I have to say. My heart is slowly falling apart, as it has been right from the start. Please take away my pain.

I Won't Be Left Behind

I run my fastest but still get beat. Land on my head when I should be on my feet. I try to move forward but I'm stuck in rewind. Why do I keep at it? I won't be left behind. The harder I'm thrown, the higher I bounce. I give it my all and that's all that counts. Some people tell me you can't and some say don't; some people give up. I reply, I won't.

Make the best of each moment the future is soon the past. The more I tell myself this, the less I come in last. Throughout my competitions I have learned what winning is about. A plain and clear lesson is giving up is the easy way out.

Every night before I go to bed I hope in a small way I have shined. Tomorrow is a brand new day and I won't be left behind.

A Piece of My Mind

I'm lost and confused. All the people I love and trusted just up and abandoned me when I needed them most. I sit here thinking about it and it all makes sense. They tried to help me but I didn't help myself. Then I realized that it was my fault, not my family's fault, but mine. I could come home drunk or stoned and when my gran would try to explain to me how much harm I was inflicting on my family, I would blow up and start punching holes through the wall or yelling and swearing, being verbally abusive.

Then I would leave the house and go find someone who was drinking. It didn't matter who it was, sometimes I would stay out for 4 or 5 days.

Since the age of 4, I was moved to different homes and different families. Finally, I got to the point where nobody was family and I didn't give a shit about anything or anybody. I've got a lot of criminal charges to be dealt with, and I don't have a home to go back to.

I'm trying to make things better. I'm trying to turn my life around. Somebody once told me, the hardest journey is from your heart to your mind. If you don't change directions, you'll end up where you're headed. In each passing minute is another chance to turn your life around for the better. And I'm trying to do all that.

Misery

I'm touched physically but mentally these streets cripple me. Witnessing misery in my history, pride hurt critically before I was born. Thanked momma for what I got cause my daddy was gone and grandma's crying asking why I gave my life to the streets; checking my forehead as if I took the mark of the beast.

Although I'm a rebel, I'm nowhere near possessed by the devil. My love for the street life got me digging my own grave with a shovel but I can't be another lost soul for this earth to claim.

It's not fair to disregard my momma's tears. She had dreams of waking up and her boy not being there. I stare in the face of death constantly. I swear it's like the grim reapers haunting me and I think that he might just catch up.

If the concrete could speak, it's no question what it would leak … who robbed who? Who shot who? Who acts tough when they are weak? When I was younger, seen my daddy sitting in jail, and I knew right there I was born to fail. I gave these streets my all and in return my reward was me witnessing my own damn fall. Life as a 'G' I blend among the frozen hearted; grew up with cockroaches all around like my bro's apartment. I wear a smile trying to cover up the pain inside. As a troubled youth I was fascinated by money and drugs, I saw my childhood say goodbye. Loving the streets with all my heart got me nothing.

Gang Life

As soon as I got into the back of that cop car in shackles and cuffs, I thought for sure there was no going back. Misery and lies and violent crimes, I can hardly bear to look into mamma's eyes without telling a lie. Only god knows if I'm going to survive. I always told my little sister, I'm right behind you, but I left her side. Now she's in the same place as me serving jail time. It ain't nothing close to paradise, so if you want my advice, I suggest you think twice.

My life is nothing close to paradise and I pray for a better way. A suicidal drug life I know all about that. I have flashbacks of me trying to take my own life, and forgetting about all the people who love me. Drowning in my fears, I was digging my own grave with a 40 caliber in my right hand, ready to take my life away. I hate thinking about that day.

Gang life really got a hold of me, but it gets cold and lonely. Getting released from custody isn't about pride in what you've done.

It is time to realize life isn't a game but who is you to blame. When you're just putting your life to shame, gang life feels like a game, but all this pain doesn't feel like a game anymore. I'm leaving the blood life.

Doing Time

The time I wasted is my biggest regret, spent in these places I'll never forget. Sitting and thinking about the things I've done, the crying and laughing, the hurt and the fun. Now it's just me, and my hard driving guilt, behind a wall of emptiness I allowed to be built.

I'm trapped in my body just wanting to run back to my childhood with its laughter and fun, but the chase is over and there's no place to hide. Everything's gone including my pride. I'm scared, alone, and stuck in this place.

Now memories of the past flash through my head, the pain is obvious by the tears I shed. I ask myself why and where I went wrong. I guess I was weak when I should have been strong. Living for drugs and the wings I had grown, my feelings were lost and afraid to be shown. As I look at my past, it's so easy to see, the fear I had, afraid to be me. I'd pretend to be rugged, so fast, so cool, when actually I'm lost like a blinded fool.

I'm getting too old for this tiresome game, of acting real hard with no sense of shame. I just live for the day when I'll get a new start, and the dreams I still hold deep in my heart. I hope I can make it, at least have to try, because I'm heading towards death and I don't want to die.

A Change

This morning I woke up and I sensed something had changed but it was nothing I could see; nothing was rearranged. For some unexplained reason when I looked in the mirror, even though the image was the same I could see myself a little clearer. My hair was just as frizzy but it didn't matter it's just hair. I still had curves in all the wrong places, but for some reason I didn't care. For once I felt just perfect, and I realized the change wasn't outside, but rather in my heart.

Incarceration: My First Time

Sitting in a sheriff's van, I was thinking of so many things at once. I would never have thought that I would ever end up in jail. I was totally being someone I wasn't. Deep down inside, I could just feel all these flowing emotions were all coming so fast. I don't think I really knew how to handle them. This was what I knew was going to be the first step of a new life. I felt kind of comfortable with it at first because it's like a whole new rush. It's like the same rush you get when you are about to fight someone. By the time I settled in, I realized that this is not a place for me. I started thinking about how hurting it was that I got caught and how deep inside I felt like things were going to start to get worse. I started missing my family a lot and missed chilling with my friends. I was so excited to get out. When I finally did, I told myself that I am better than that. I will never come back. Now look where I am!

I know I'm smarter than this but for some reason I just keep coming back. This time, when I get out, I hope that I will never have to feel those feelings that I felt ever again. Some advice is do something with your life, don't be a 'lifer.' There is way more to life than jail. Life is supposed to be something worth living for, so live it!

Jail

What does it mean to be in jail, what is it like to have no freedom. All 1 have ever known is to fail, thinking if I write poems will people even read them? To me I'm dead, to others I'm dying. I've messed up my own life this I'm not denying. Some days I want to die, some days I want to live. Some days I want to take and others I want to give. I can't completely explain my thoughts, because of all these blurry spots.

This place will change your life forever. It will leave you with thoughts; feeling blind and severed. Some people say jail is like daycare, but the mental damage it will inflict will stay there forever. People can't just tell you what jail is like, because most will say it's easy, like riding a bike. They will leave out what would really count; this would leave out a large amount. It's hard to say the damage it has done, but I'll tell you one thing, it ain't no fun.

All I want is to walk outside, but by jail rules I must abide. I now live my life for a second chance. Most days feel like I'm stuck in a trance. Some days I feel I could cry, there it goes dripping from the corner of my eye. But my time will soon come, where I can live once more. Where I can go outside and have fun, or even walk to the store. People take advantage of freedom and how great it is. Trust me I did too but for my second chance I live. Jail is cold and dark, not a pretty sight. I cannot find my spark; at the end of my tunnel there is no light. This is jail in here no one will prevail.

Freedom

I look outside the window of my cell and I see pretty blue skies, birds chirping, sunshine, and the first word that pops in my head is freedom. I take my eyes away from the outside and look around my cell. All I see inside my room is cold, dreary brick walls that seem to be closing in on me, and a hard bed with one thin mattress thrown on top and stuck to the ugly brick wall. There's only one word that fits the description of this place, hell.

Hell to me is a place where you don't get to see your friends or family. You have to ask when to do this and that, you even have to ask permission when you need to go to the washroom. I look back out my window, and then back in my cell. Yes, I think I'd rather choose freedom.

Hope

I'm getting out pretty soon, and for the first time I have hope and faith that I can succeed on the outside and never come back here. I have been in and out of jail since I was 13, and now I'm 18. This last time, I finally realized that I don't want that kind of life for myself. I realized that family is more important than drugs, alcohol, crime, or my so-called 'friends.' And if I continue doing dumb shit, I will lose either my family or my life.

My priorities have also changed. All I used to care about before was getting drunk, high, or having fun doing whatever I wanted, even though I was hurting everyone around me. Now all I care about is spending time with family, going to school, graduating, and making something out of myself. Everyone has endless potential and before I came in here, 1 was selling myself short, the same as a lot of people in here are doing. I only hope and pray that each and every one of you in here finds their potential and purpose, before it's too late. Straighten out your lives, don't do it for anyone, do it for yourself.

Tomorrow

The day has come for me to be free and yes I can change the way things will be. I know it gets hard, but I will stay strong and prove to everyone I could all along. I want to apologize to everyone I've hurt.

Everything I've done in the past makes me feel lower than dirt. I want to be happy and not sit in sorrow, because my new life will start tomorrow.

List some of the things you will do on that first day.

Horror-scopes

Libra (Sept 24 – Oct 23)

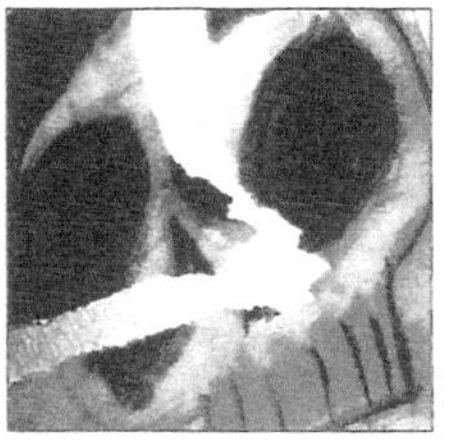

Unfortunately, the moon, sun, and earth are lined up perfectly, which could possibly mean 24 hour lockdowns will be passed out to you like candy.

Scorpio (Oct 24 – Nov 22)

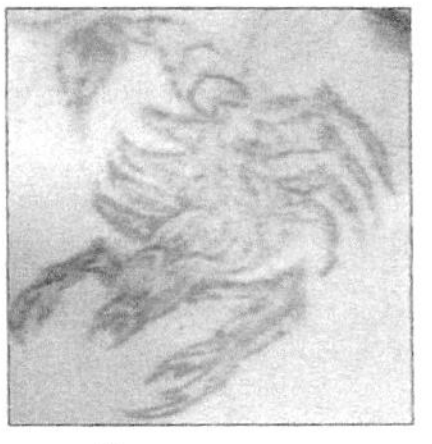

After a reading of the stars, it was found out Mr. Yagger possibly lost more hair than usual and could drop you to a level one-meals out.

Sagittarius (Nov 23 – Dec 21)

Everyone wants to be a critic. Everyone wants to have their say. This could be you. But a new instated law brought to us by VYCC says no one cares.

Capricorn (Dec 22 – Jan 20)

Pluto and Uranus have collided so get rid of all contraband because they will probably suspect you as the culprit and rooms will be tossed.

Figure U5.2 Victoria Youth Custody Centre (VYCC), "Horror-scopes"

Inside on My 16th Birthday

And where do I find myself in this sixteenth year of living? I'm not the person I thought I would be, it was me, who I was kidding. Where am I now? My sixteenth summer is passing, and I sit here, gloomy, wondering and asking myself where will I go and who will I be, beyond these walls of brick?

Thinking of the things I've done is enough to make me sick. Life is but a trick and I'm ever a failure. My stomach churns and my face grows paler. What is life like beyond these walls? I've forgotten so much, almost forgotten it all, what will it be like to live life without restrictions? It will feel nothing short of crazy to make my own decisions.

Although for now it's been a fantasy vision. Wonderful is the day I can look around and not have a fence caging me in. Beautiful is the moment I'm free from this stress aging me, but it will be different, so very sad in a way, when I leave this place and say goodbye someday, because although it's been a burden, it became a comfort zone, because in here I'm taken care of and don't feel so alone. Sometimes I get scared of getting out and being on my own. The life I was living wore me down and was too risky. Sometimes I don't want to try anymore; don't want to cry anymore. Mad at the world and it's getting worse, I'm sick of feeling like I'm living a curse. So where will I go and who will I be? I guess in the end it's all up to me.

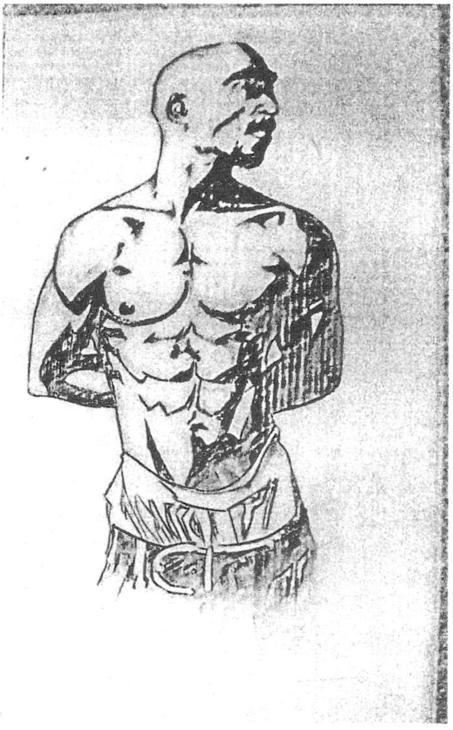

Figure U5.3 Victoria Youth Custody Centre (VYCC), C.D., 'Tupac' drawing and wood burning on panel

The writers in Unit 5 reflected on their lives and the strength it takes to make life changes.

Discussion

Can people change?

Do you know someone who has changed for the better? What helped them?

Write about something you would like to change about yourself or your life.

What are some of the obstacles that prevent you from obtaining your goals?

Identify aspects of your life (e.g., a childhood experience that evokes a strong memory, a story a grandparent or friend told you).

Drugs and Violence

Figure U6.1 Photograph, Victoria Youth Custody Centre (VYCC), six of *The Outside Guide* researchers
Photograph by Carol Cross.

Hope: On Life's Terms

What is this thing we call drug addiction? Our lives revolve around it, but still there is no clear cure. Deprivation, death, sorrow, these are the things we get out of it. And yet it feels like home; our minds corrupted by this man-made substance that can make us think and feel invincible.

Loneliness and unloved is what we know. Hate and violence is what we do, but things can change. The next feeling might be of hope and courage but yet it all gets washed away with the next hit. Why do we do this to ourselves? Why did I do this to myself?

I've seen death, felt deprivation, and witnessed sorrow. Life seems worthless, but yet now I feel hope. This hope gets me through the day and hopefully, tomorrow.

So for anyone who has this disease of addiction, just remember, that even though you seem at the bottom, it's only a few steps further to the top

What are your hopes for the future?

What visual images could communicate this well? If you can, gather images of yourself that identify your skills, beliefs, values, and future goals. This could be a collage of images from magazines, your drawings, or journal notes ... your ongoing project.

The Drugs and the Streets

It's weird how shit happens. All these youths with no homes, and broken hearts; drug pheens on the street with no food or shoes on their feet. Just to get by you have to cheat and lie. Most people can't do it, they just panic and die.

Diseases spread and multiply. People want to escape reality so they take drugs to affect their mentality; almost always ends in fatality. It starts with weed. You get really hungry and you need to feed. You take on that smoke until you choke, too lazy to get a job so you're flat broke. All your money spent on munchies and dope, so you start selling drugs like coke. You hear it's an awesome high, so you give it a try. You think you're superman because you feel like you can fly. You don't realize that soon you're going to die. Now you're an addict for crack. You're smoking it out back in a shack. Then you hear of smack. First you snort it then you inject it. Blood to blood contact, now you're infected. You try to live in a normal society, but you've been rejected. You resort to prostitution as a solution. Life for you is just an illusion. You're considered a whore and the pimp you work for says you're no good anymore. You soon decide your only option is suicide, but no one cares or cries because it's just another junkie who has died.

Little do they realize you were once a beautiful baby. They can't hear you screaming 'save me.' Someone who was once a person's miracle has now become someone who's hysterical. It brings nothing but pain to know, troubled youths having nothing but drugs to gain.

Alone

I was alone the first time I put that clear glass pipe to my lips.

I was alone the numerous times I sat in the alley and smoked gram upon gram of shard.

I was alone as I sat awake at night higher than kite holding myself wishing that those were another's arms wrapped tightly but ever so gently around my body.

I was alone as I walked the streets with my shades hiding my red puffy eyes after a long session of crying.

I was alone as I stood on the corner yelling up, down, crack, smack just so I could eat one decent meal a day.

I was alone every time those good old handcuffs got slapped on, and that big inescapable door got slammed behind me.

I was alone the first day I raised the glass to my mouth.

And I'm alone now as I lay here quietly in my room and listen to the recurrent sounds of cell doors banging closed behind others who are in the same place as me.

I was alone; I am alone!

Drugs

You might think at the time you're having fun, but don't realize how much damage is being done. From smoking a joint or snorting a rail, doing these drugs, you can end up in jail.

You might think this is a joke, but you won't be laughing after you're totally broke. Now it's time to get more, stealing, cheating, robbing, lying, beating, whatever it takes as long as you score. Don't get me wrong, not all druggies are bad, but if you ask me, the lifestyle is sad.

Now for all you drinkers ... alcohol's a drug too, everything from hard stuff down to homemade brew. Booze is legal, but drinking too much will change your brain. You can be the nicest person to going literally insane. Some people lose everything, even family and friends. Stay clean you know what I mean?

Crystal Meth

Have you ever done something that you hated all your life; thought about it with hate knowing it took your Mom's life and wishing you could kill it but it's not really a living thing. It's taking over this world; taking away innocent lives. I despise this drug. I pray for a remedy to help this world.

Once wanted to try something new, but what a fluke it almost took my life. I was set about the crime and now it's jail time. My addictions got worse and I felt no remorse. This drug became a physical need for me. I felt like a walking zombie waiting for more hits. Crystal meth really got a hold of me.

Walking alone along the Vancouver streets at night, my physical appearance at the time was not a great sight. Alone, confused, being sexually abused, seeking help was something I had refused. My legs scarred from the constant picking, all I could think about was getting my next hit. Hastings, Kingsway, Broadway, they're all the same to me. Prostitute is what my addiction has forced me to be. Why must I keep treating myself the same? A healthy lifestyle is what I now must obtain.

One Minute

One minute I'm just chilling having fun. The next my life is over—done. My life spun out of control and now I'm stuck in this hellhole. People think I'm crazy well can you blame me? If I locked you up and threw away the key wouldn't you be? I sit in my cell day after day, keeping silent all I have to say, I keep inside all the pain I feel thinking this can't be real.

One minute I'm chilling having fun, the next my life is over. Some girl thought she was tough, wanted to fight, started to get rough, she took a shot and missed, the last thing she saw was my fist. Next thing you know 3 girls surround me, things start to look real ugly. The 3 girls tried to lynch me, so I took out my shank and said come and get me. Then there's blood everywhere and the one girl she was just lying there, her throat slit, her friends screaming, having a hissy fit. All I could do was stare, trying to get the blood out of my hair. Then it hit me, oh my god, the police tried to question me, but all I could do was nod. One minute I'm chilling, having fun, the next my life is over. Done.

Life on the Streets

The life on the streets I'm tired of doing it; the ways of the drugs too young to play with. Wound up in the hole far too many times; I can't live like this no more. I try to change but it's all I know. I'm so numb to the pain. I haven't cried in years, and through it all I just sat and ignored my fears. Depression I can't take it no more. I'm tired of hearing 'girl, what's wrong with you go get some help.' Do I want to change? I do but I need help and some support from you.

I Am Alcohol

I'm a powerful substance; give me a try. I'll give you courage and strength, no need to feel shy. You're at a party and you want to look good so grab me and pop off my top just like I knew you would. You take a big swig, not caring how much you take. Now I got you under my spell, no chance to escape; I change the way you act. I change the way you think; all because you took one little drink. You are powerless over me, you know it is true. You think you look good, but you're acting like a fool.

You've done stupid things that you wish you could change. You stay out late; your school grades are going down the drain. One day you're drinking with your buddies, you decide to take a drive. You feel on top of the world, you feel alive. Everything is blurry, you can barely see. Boy, you're having fun, it doesn't seem like reality. You floor the gas pedal, without thinking twice, not even knowing you're risking your life. You think you see a car ahead, you're not so sure. You can't get a grasp on the wheel you're starting to swerve. You hit the curb and flipped to the side. Now if you could go back would you still have tried?

Letter to My Dearest Self (Drugs)

You're probably losing touch with who you are right now— and you need a reminder. A reminder of all the problems drugs and poor decisions have caused for you in the past. Drugs and alcohol haven't been good friends to you. They are thieves. They've taken away your freedom, your family, your girlfriend, your school, sports, and your friends.

They have caused a significant amount of damage to your self. They have made you forget about your sterling qualities and they made you believe that you are a loser. They robbed you of your self-respect. They tried to convince you that crime was ok and that the badass lifestyle was for you. Drugs are a trick and are not a solution to anything.

Remember, the only real way through a problem is to solve it. Focusing on the trouble or problem is a dark pit, a limitless abyss. Focus on the solutions. Solutions are sometimes hard and are about doing the right thing. You're probably trying to escape from your own wisdom at this time. You are likely conning yourself, lying to yourself, trying to make deals with yourself, trying to minimize the power and destruction that drugs, booze, and crime have wrecked on you and your life.

You're probably saying just this once and it will be ok — I will get away with it. Bullshit, you are fooling yourself. You must remember what the cost has been so far. Do you really want to pay that bill again? If you choose to go down that path again, it may not be a friendly place that you land on. Take a minute and look around you. Realize where you are and imagine where you want to be. Remember your goals; remember your hopes; remember your loved ones. And even if it doesn't seem like it right now, people love you, care for you, value you, and want you to do good.

Today I (add your name) *stand for freedom, wellbeing, and happiness. I stand for being a better person and not feeling ashamed of myself. Do you really want to take that away? I am curious about learning and growing as a person. Don't turn that hope off! Drugs, booze, and crime aren't the way to get there.*

Minutes Like Hours (A Fatal Day with Alcohol)

You walk into the store, and stride down the aisle. You pick me up and try to look casual while you carry me down to the checkout line, pull out your wallet, you soon will be mine. Your friends are observing every move that you make. The clerk asks for ID, you show him a fake. You quickly walk to the front of the store and your friends are waiting for you as you step out the door. You hop in the car and drive away from the shop, shut off the ignition, and pop off my top. You take a few drinks and pass me around. That's when you decide to take a drive around town. You turn on your car and put your foot to the clutch. I'm sober, you think, I didn't have very much. You pull onto the road with me by your side; take occasional sips as you enjoy the ride. Then the brakes on the car in front of you squeal. You try hard to stop but you lost control of the wheel. You skid off the road and you know you have crashed, the dashboard is shattered; the windshield is smashed. Minutes like hours, you're in treacherous pain that washes your senses, envelopes your brain. The screams all around you are faint to your ears, as life flashes before you, your hopes and your fears. Minutes like hours you plead and you pray, I'll never touch it again, just let me live one more day. Your mind starts to go dark and it falls apart; then slip into blackness, the pain has ceased. Before you entered the store you should have thought twice, for I am the substance that cost you your life!

Men Don't Cry

I don't cry because my mom told me men don't cry.

Now I keep my feelings in by staying high. All the stuff I been through, I don't talk about it, or cry about it. I wash it away by getting high. It's probably the things that have been done to me in the past; my heart just went cold. Well, I was high and drunk going 100 down the highway. Then woke up in city cells trying to figure out what happened. Going to court for a stolen car and I don't remember.

Now I'm back inside prison trying to hold the tears in; trying to find out what went wrong. So I lay down in my cell and write why I can't cry, and why do I lie to the people that love and care for me?

My Song

She was always a happy girl but if you look hard enough you can see that she has a lot of pain and anger, but she tried to run away from this anger hoping that she'll never have to look back.

Making herself drink until she was pass buzzed, wondering what she did or whose house that was. Because of her boyfriend's problems, she even turned to drugs without knowing what she was doing, but she didn't care, she hated life. That is why she grabbed the knife, thinking that she would die that night because everybody she knew would just tell her lies saying everything was going to be all right. Tears swiftly running down her face she had lost all faith.

The life I've been living has been way too crazy. I don't want to be in a world of hate, pain, and lies mixed with lonely cries. My life is messed up, it's just a bad dream now, but somebody please wake me up.

Violence: Is It Worth It?

Sometimes violence seems like the only way, but when you're involved this could be your last day. Sometimes you sit and think, I wish I never sealed my fate. Now everything seems in slow motion with blood so thick pouring out like an ocean. I feel so weak, but at the same time so strong, just wondering how this all went so wrong.

I should have stayed home even if I was left all alone. The only thing I now wish is to give my mom just one last kiss and tell her I'm sorry for all the years I will miss. But I won't have the chance; I won't have the time. What if I had changed my mind? I should have just stayed home, but now I'm dying in here alone.

Desperation

I can hear the desperate whimpering of a junkie, rig in hand, trying desperately to find a vein; it's more than she can stand. I can see the look of confusion drugs bring as she pours another drink, trying desperately to numb herself so she doesn't have to think. I can no longer stand to look in the mirror; she's finally out of control. I can no longer stand to see or hear the mirrored reflection of my soul.

My Biggest Regret

Help me, I am lost, I don't know what to do or who to turn to. I don't know who to love or who to be loyal to. I don't know what I should do, so I turn to alcohol and drugs for help but it seems to make my problems worse. I used more and more, and my problems got bigger and bigger. Some people say I'm just a lost soul right now. And maybe I am I'm not sure myself, nobody can really be sure. There is a small light of hope deep inside of me somewhere. I cannot find it right now because it is smothered in all my hatred and anger, all my pain, all my fears, and my problems. I am lost. Help me somebody. Please find me, love me, and care for me. Please be there for me when I need you most. Please be there for me when I need to talk to you, I need you. I need your help.

Emotions (A Response)

Sometimes when I'm sad or stressed out, I will turn to alcohol and drugs for help but that only escalates my problems. But when I've found out that works better than turning to alcohol and drugs is little things like drawing, writing, listening to music, or talking to somebody. Somebody you can trust to be there for you. Somebody who will listen to you or take a walk or bike ride with you. And when you talk to somebody, it doesn't always have to be family. Just somebody you can trust which is a whole lot better than smoking weed or slamming a forty. Some of you might think otherwise, but you probably don't see how much damage both alcohol and drugs inflict upon you and others around you such as your family, plus your community that you live with. It was Pat R. that wrote 'Finding Community.' It pretty much explains how important the community really is, but you have to belong to the right community. I know I never really saw how much harm I was causing my community for a long time. That's why I'm trying to change my lifestyle. It's not that easy; simpler said than done. It's hard to change your lifestyle, but someone once told me that in each passing minute is another chance to turn it all around for the better.

Out There

There are people who would kill without a second thought. Out there, there are people whose souls are long sold and bought.

You see the world through such happy eyes, but see the way that woman cries? Out there men aren't always nice, it's not all sugar and spice. I haven't seen it all, but I've seen enough to know, out there really isn't any place you want to go. Out there nothing comes cheap, there are secrets you have to keep. It starts small then grows big and I lived it every day. I know enough not to ever go back there.

Out there it's long nights and cold days. You'll kill yourself with all your shame, no one's to blame, but out there it never gets better only worse. Trust me, I know I've lived this curse. But I caught myself before I fell too hard. Don't smoke that shard it'll ruin you. It'll claim your soul and mind.

Don't do drugs, you won't be you anymore. You'll throw everything out the door to get more. Don't ever let a man treat you any less than gold. Remain brave and bold, because out there it's as dark as night. Stay in the light because once you have lost it, it's hard to get back. What I'm telling you is true. Make sure your past won't be something you're ashamed to look at.

My Life

It's hard to live this life of mine from making regretful choices from doing stupid crimes. It is hard going though teenage stages from experiencing drugs, from going through fazes. You snort or drink to ease your problems away, but it just makes your problems stay; you want to stop but at the same time you want more, your head is pounding, your nose is sore ... so before you make that choice, think how precious you are. You don't need drugs to make you feel like a star.

In Unit six, teens wrote about their reality with drugs and violence.

Is someone you know struggling with substance abuse? Maybe a family member or close friend?

Write them a letter or make a drawing describing your feelings. Choose words or details to catch the mood of what you see and experience.

Select an experience that you are comfortable to share.

Unit 7

Love and Loss

Figure U7.1 Drawing on wood with burning, feathers, and acrylic paint, by W.E.

Free to Fly

Free in the sky I see your soul fly, and it hurts me deep inside. You were filled with joy and happiness, that is why it will be you I miss. It's hard to believe that you are gone, because in your eyes there was a beautiful song. Our hearts ache and no one will be the same.

Love is something that is in you to give, and once you feel it you never want that feeling to go away. You get to the point where you're so in love that you will do anything for that feeling that you once felt. If you lose that feeling, I guess sometimes it can get to the point where there is nothing left in life worth living for. If that love falls apart, what would you do? Would you start over? Would you put as many memories as you can into a box and keep it locked forever to never forget? There are so many different ways to explain love. Love is a strong word and so are your feelings.

Suicide Note (Crimson Tears)

If you're reading this then I finally did it, I'm sorry I didn't say goodbye, there was no time. Understand I was stressed, living day to day was hard, but I gave it my best until there was nothing left. Don't you shed no tears just remember all the good times we had over the years. Never cry, never think bad of me, what is done is done and that's the way it had to be.

All this time you never knew what I was feeling; now you lay awake staring at the ceiling. If you can't sleep at night, don't worry about me I'm alright.

Tears caress my face. Blood drips down my arm. Slice, slice, slice is my little game of self-harm. Now my body's raw, searching through my mind I had found a little flaw. There is nothing left. The drugs make it worse. Doctors get paid and mind games are played. Then I found you in all your grace lying there with a smirk on your face. A ring of crimson circles around you on the floor and a dull black 22 is on the floor. Now you're dead at 16 years and I sit on the floor alone crying my crimson tears.

When I Die

My strength ebbs away, like the ocean tide. I lay dying as night falls like rain on my island home.

Crabs scatter across the stones. When I die, remember to bury me with my father in the cool dark forest.

To Love

To love each other from brother to brother, and don't ever forget you only have 1 mother.

Respect your 2 parents and your whole family; it'll help cure a soul so you can be free.

Live by the rules and do the best you can. Have faith in yourself; rise to be a man.

Figure U7.2 Wooden chest, by T.

A man with respect with a life and a goal; now there is something a thief never stole.
It can't be stolen, for it lives deep inside.
And when you find it, don't ever let go. Hold onto it tight and enjoy the show!

Figure U7.3 Drawing, wood burning on panel, by T.

Describe a person that you love.

A Letter for Larry

Today I thought about you, my dear friend. You were up in the skies, living the life that doesn't end and just as always, you had a smile on your face. The smile that we all remember you showing. You used to come see me every Friday and we would exchange each other's thoughts. We'd tell each other our truths, our lies, and each other's beliefs at no cost.

Whenever I was down, you would always tell me that everything's going to be all right. And you I had to believe, because it was truly only you who was right. I didn't get the chance to say goodbye. And forever in my life, I will always wonder why. If only I could get just one last exchange. Just one last Friday with you and I would share with you the last of my secrets, and tell you how much I will truly miss you.

I remember the day that I found out of your passing away. The words came out of her mouth and I really did not know what to say. And sadness was the only thing that filled the rest of my day, because I had no one left to talk to, on this Friday. Rest in peace, buddy, with love.

You Will Always Be in My Heart R.I.P.

This cannot be happening. You were like my sister, a part of my heart. It just breaks to know you're gone. I just want to cry and hug someone. Without you everything for me is falling apart. I just want to be free and start a new life. You think it's easy, it's not, my friend tried, but she died at age 17.

The chilling sound of your blood as it falls. I watch your head bounce off the wall. You were here but now you're gone, never right but always wrong. Where is my love, I have no more. I found you there on the bathroom floor. Cannot speak cuz of fears, cannot see cuz of tears. Cannot write cuz of shakes, and this is where my story breaks. In loving memory.

Figure U7.4 North Coast Wolf, acrylic on paper, by Anon

Some Days (I'm a Parent)

On some days I sit staring out the window watching this world pass me by. Sometimes I think there's nothing to live for, and I almost break down and cry.

Some days I feel like the world is on my shoulders and everyone's leaning on me, but then she comes back to me. My baby girl keeps getting older and I watch her grow with pride. I'm sorry that I hurt you, but soon I'll be with you and looking at your face.

Writing / Art Exercise

Think about something you have always wanted to say to someone you care about. This could be a close friend, child, or family member, but you never had the opportunity to say it.

Illustrate your words with a drawing.

Relationships

Figure U8.1 Pencil on paper, by A.M.

Friendship

Take my hand, dear friend. Chase away my doubts and fears and wipe the tears from off my face. Friend, I cannot stand alone; I need your hand to hold.

The warmth of your gentle touch in my world that's grown cold. Please be a friend to me and hold me day to day, because with your loving hand in mine I know we'll find the way.

What makes a good friend?

Becoming a Parent: A Promise to My Child

My child, you have the right to be born as perfect as possible. I will help you grow and nourish us both. I will keep us from harm, the harm of alcohol, the harm of drugs, the harm of careless living, and the harm of violent ways. You will not be born into a perfect world, but you will be born perfectly you, as perfect as only you can be. This is my promise to you. I ask the creator and all the powers of good on this earth and of the spirit world to guide and assist me.

Abuse

I always want one word to never exist; that word is abuse. Everywhere you look, there's abuse: drug abuse, alcohol abuse, sexual abuse. Every time I look at the sky, I wish someday I would just die because of my childhood, I've had every kind of abuse from family or friends. I know about abuse.

When you phoned and begged me back, my mind went blank. I didn't know what to say or think. The only thing that popped into my mind was all the memories of the things you had done to me. You hurt me and made me cry. You ruined my life and I could never ever go back to that life.

Why Does It Hurt to Love You? (A Letter to My Mom)

As I'm walking down the street, I see a mother and daughter with the best friendship I've ever seen, and it hurts me because you are not here to have that with. I also ask myself, why does it hurt to love you? If I could, I'd answer that question myself. One thing that worries me is your wealth and your health. Yes, I love you dearly with all my heart but it hurts so bad. I don't know if it's right or wrong to feel this way about loving you. Just thinking about you makes me mad because I'm also so very hurt and sad.

I'm not sure if this is reality, or if it's just anger I feel. This isn't a choice I'm just using my voice. I haven't seen you in two years, and this poem just makes me want to burst out in tears. If you were my kid and I was your mother, you would be under my roof, not any other. Answer me one question, because you have the choice, would you change if I did it for you? Because you need to know you have the choice, otherwise the addiction is just going to keep you going. And to know people care, you feel that much better. But if you keep letting the drugs take over your mind, you are going to keep telling yourself that no one cares. And then the drugs will soon take your life. From the day you left, to this very day, I still ask myself, why does it hurt to love you.

My Kind of Love

The kindness in your heart has taken away my pain. You have made me so happy, even at the sound of your name. I am truly lucky to have found a person like you and I feel I can trust you with everything.

You have made my life better; I don't know how to thank you. You put a smile on my face even after all we've been through. You never left my side; you've always stood strong.

Through the tough times you've shown me that we truly belong. Sometimes in life things may not always go our way, but our love for one another is growing stronger each day.

You have made my blue skies bright, and touched deeply my heart. Deep down we know nothing will tear us apart.

Figure U8.2 "Thunderbird and Salmon," acrylic on paper, by T.

Trauma and Pain

I walk home knowing the inevitable, and just as I suspected she is seated upon the couch waiting. My heart begins to speed as she screams and threatens to beat me with whatever she can grasp. I know it is coming, so I curse her and walk to my room. As I wait for her to come, a sudden calm comes over me. I've experienced it many times before.

The door opens and as I look upon her hand, my heart stops, for she is not alone, instead she is accompanied by an electric cord so tightly wrapped around her hand, it looks as if it would split a table at the thrust of her arm. As I take the punishment, I can feel the blood dripping down my flesh, and I still refuse to cry. Once she is done, I look at her with coldness in my eyes and I spit. She realizes what she has done and walks out of my room with blood dripping down the weapon that caused me so much pain.

As soon as she leaves, I climb out of my window and begin to run. All I hear is my feet hitting the wet pavement. I make it to town and people stare. I am covered in blood and I'm missing my shirt. But I don' t care, for I know what I have to do and I set out to do it. As the night grows colder, I stare down to the cold water 200 feet below and I jump. I am falling.

I begin to remember my life and remember how she raised me, and I appreciate everything she has done. I now remember that I love her and no wounds could suppress this and I'll do whatever it takes to remember her in the next life, because this woman gave me life. She is and always will be my mother.

My Father

The hatred I have for my father adds up to the amount I love him. I have no feelings for this man that spread his seed to create me. I only have wonder. My wonder is how could a man watch his son be born and then depart his life like a train would a station? He is like a nomad in the desert only he keeps returning to places he has already been to ruin lives even more. Spreading his seed from woman to woman; creating an army of children with hate and that only have dreams of darkness, until one day these children turn on him. At the end this man will die lonely, and the only lady he will have will be lady heroin. I can only imagine what this man thinks, for he too is a foot soldier in a war that only addicts know. Everything I've told you is the truth, that is who he is, an addict, once my hero … my father.

I'll Be Free

I've shed my tears until there were none, tried to stop them, but they continued to run. Thought life was good but it really was not what it seemed. I'm going to make it though and accomplish my dream. Not too much longer before I may finally be free, and be there for my boy and girl, whom I look forward again to see.

My Mom

I love my mom; I honestly do. We've been through hard situations and managed to survive. I forgave her for abandoning me and forgave her for choosing booze, drugs, and men over her own blood. I just wish she forgave herself too.

She keeps running and running but when she stops, she has to run again. It makes me so sad. Broken promises and broken trust but I'm still there. I'll always be there, but where is she when I need love and support? No matter what she does to me or to herself, I'm here for her even though she causes so much sadness.

Discussion

If you have witnessed or experienced an incident of violence at your school or in your community, take a moment to write about it, and if you can, share with the group.

Who can you contact if someone you know is experiencing an abusive relationship and needs your help?

Who can you contact if you are experiencing an abusive relationship?

How do you respond to witnessing violence either in your home life or in the community?

Who can you turn to? Or where can you go to feel safe?

Write about someone in your family who has had a strong effect on you in either a negative or a positive way. It could be a brother, an uncle, a parent who is hurtful, or someone whose hard work and kindness inspires you.

Describe this person in detail: What do they look like? Do you want to be like this person? Or would you want to be different? Why?

Choice and Having Your Say

Figure U9.1 Mural, by Tashina A. and Carol Cross (40′ × 48′)
Photograph by Carol Cross.

The reality is that sometimes we make choices regarding drug use, criminal behavior, and street life because our options in life are limited.

The World Through My Eyes

The world is my playground. East Vancouver is my back yard. From almost as far back as I can remember, from the moment I woke up to the time I went to sleep, I watched my back and hustled my way through and just hoped I would make it one more day. Welfare didn't pay enough for my family to eat, so I resorted to crime to eat and feed my family.

All this unnecessary violence of kids fighting and joining gangs to find a place of belonging, and families fighting other families for the block to hustle and earn a living. Drama dwells thicker than the smog of pollution that floods the streets where we live, and blazing clouds our mind to cover up our emotions. Drinking, doing drugs to escape reality, smoking weed to get high so we can leave this place, our problems, and just float off into space.

Writing Exercise

This is space for *your* self- reflection.

The world through my eyes:

Some teens are faced with life's obstacles and personal histories of abuse and neglect. The following story suggests wanting to make changes but needing support in order to make those right choices.

A Gangster Life

If you want to be a child of the devil, all you have to do is hand over your soul. Don't be scared, I thought you were a rebel! I thought being a gangster was your goal. You seem like you had a fright, buck up gangster don't cry, pull the trigger tighter. I don't want to hear the question why. Don't you want to be hardcore? Well to be that you have to kill a man. Don't follow your heart, just ignore it and trust me. Listen to the plan, kill, lie, and cheat. Listen to your leader and big deal if your life is incomplete; to the devil you're just another bottom feeder. You want to turn back too bad your soul belongs to him. If you try to escape he'll attack and when he catches you it will be grim. With the devil all you will do is fail.

Reflecting Back

For the past two years I've been coming here, and when I get out I'll be 18 years old and off probation. I'm going to do something productive with my life, instead of committing crimes. I'll be getting a job … no more run-ins with law enforcement. When I look around, all I see is natives. It's time to start proving to ourselves and to our parents that we aren't stupid or good for nothing. Life can be good and of course, hard. Live your life; be someone and prove them all wrong. Even if you have people that doubt you can change, keep good goals and stay strong!

Runaway

I'm done living my life in the fast lane. It's about time I break this criminal chain. I was always told I would never amount to shit. Even my teachers told me to give up and quit. So I did, I dropped out. I ran away from home and never said bye. Now I'm on the streets slinging these drugs, but wishing I was home exchanging hugs. I want to go home, but I don't know how. I want to go home, I want to go now. The sadness hurts so bad so I take another hit. There I go again, I gave up and quit.

Support

In the following story, the writer continues to write about wanting to change and needing support after spending all his teen years in jail.

Shed Tears

How can I finish life, if I don't know how to start? How can I keep living with a cold heart and how is this blood still flowing through my veins? And how do I keep ending up in these chains?

Once you're in the system, it's hard to get out, because society fills your head with nothing but doubt. I need my family and my family needs me but I'm sitting in prison when I could be free. Is this my last sentence, am I really done, or will I get out and just start to run?

No, this is it, I'm done wasting my time; I don't need to live a life of crime. I have wasted well over seven years and all I have to show are these shed tears.

Deep inside I try not to cry, as I watch myself get older and just watch this time pass by. I want a chance to start my life over and become someone new. Forget all my past life, and just do what I got to do. I want to stand strong and tall, and just keep it real every time I am about to fall. I am tired of feeling alone, sitting by myself staring at everything that I own. I want to be able to keep myself in line, and be with someone that forever is mine. I want to promise myself the chance at a new way. But also I want to give myself one last promise … the promise of a new day!

Words from 'Inside'

As I listen to this old school beat I think about the days I was running on the street. Thinking selling drugs was so cool, real neat, now I'm tweaking in the jail crying in defeat. All I did was lie, thieve, deceit, from this whole lifestyle and profile I'll retreat. Living life ruthless isn't good, isn't fun. Plus your mind's always hazed when you are living on the run. Now I spit lyrics outta my mouth like a gun, and in this competition, I know we won, that's it, it's done. Only way I did it is with my father by my side, all this faith I have inside doesn't want to hide. All I have to do is look in time, and I start to wonder why, why I ever did crime. Just to make a couple of dimes and now I sit here bustin' rhymes, rapping to you guys snorting lines, trying to get you to turn around, and live life underground. Away from all the trouble, that's bound to land you in jail. Stacking chips to make bail. This lifestyle gets stale, so look to god to go straight. Can't you relate before your life disintegrates. And you can't go through the white gates, when you die it's not worth getting high and watching your life go by. Now you sit and wonder why you didn't even try to slow down. I hit rock bottom looking like a clown. Sitting in a cell, drowning in defeat, I didn't have to try and run the street. All I did was lie and deceit. I've got to get on my feet, and steer in the right direction. Just try with all your might to never act out of anger and spite.

Hope for the Future

I've been thinking about the many ways I've turned out. Sometimes so messed up, I couldn't see what life is really about. Living the high life, going the opposite ways of my dreams but I thought nothing of it, 'cause it didn't feel as bad as it seemed. Smoking, drinking, hooking up with them girls. I don't know about you, but this was good times in my world. But with the good times, there were always the bad.

Just like with the happy, there's always the sad; I was hurting my family; I was too blind to see. Still I had no feelings, cause I didn't know how much they loved me. Then at the lowest point of my life I finally opened my eyes.

And seen the world for what it is, and learned my truth and my lies. I've put so much time to waste. I'm going to accomplish my life goals. And just as always, there's no one that can get in my way, because I'm a lot stronger now and continue to be more every day.

Deep Breath I Take

When I sit here and think about my troublesome life, this deep breath I take I put down the knife. My restless soul waits for me to walk again, so I can hold my own amongst all these men. So helpless and weak it's all up to me, but with good friends I am able to be free. The small things in life will never be the same, but the bigger picture is still me in the game. I cannot quit now but it's tough ... now I'm so glad of those deep breaths I take.

A Journey That Will Change You

Plead guilty or not is always on my mind, there has to be one answer to find. The crime took place and yes I was there, but to the others would that be fair? With my guilty conscience on stand I would choke; I want to do the right thing, but my mind's full of smoke.

Just tell her I'm guilty, let my mind be at ease. I'll pay all my dues and pray on my knees. Plus, if I can do crime, I should do the time, but plenty of people would drop on a dime. Don't look back, look straight above, god does love you with plenty of love. He helped me with this and all sorts of things; we aren't all perfect we're human beings. He taught me things in all sorts of ways, to look past the sin and live better days.

A Devil on My Shoulder

Some say it's insanity, some say it's fear, but I say it's the little guy whispering in my ear. Telling you to do all kinds of crazy shit. And the whole time he's whispering, don't worry man, don't worry keep going you can make it to Surrey. Look, steal that car, c'mon, you know it's too far to run. Let's do it, it'll be fun. But this cop got you spun to the ground, told you not to make a sound. They found that pound of weed in your backpack so now you're in jail with no chance of bail. And that little bastard seems to never fail at getting in your head. He said, 'shitty man that you got caught, but you're lucky you never got shot, but wait till you get older.' I had to interrupt because I need to get bolder. It's time to stop listening to that devil on my shoulder.

A Parent's Time in Jail

At times I forget where I am, then I see that I'm in jail. And even though I know I deserve every last hour, I just wish that I had a chance for bail because I've created a family of my own now. And it feels as though I don't have much time. I now have kids that look up to their dad, and to wake up in jail not beside either of them makes me feel even worse than that word, sad. But I'll get through it, and I'll keep my head high. Nobody will be able to stop me. I'll stay strong, standing on these two feet of mine. There will be people who don't believe you will ever change, but in the end trust in yourself, make good choices, and you'll be better than every last one of them.

Getting Out of Jail

Once I get out, I always head back, selling my poison straight outta the shack, stab people for fun and my boys be 'like that's whack,' my life revolved around buying and selling crack.

My life contained violence and drugs; constantly around gangsters and thugs. I don't know, maybe when I was a kid I needed a few extra hugs. I once had a real job but then I quit, for the good life I just didn't seem fit. So I said no to the world of being legit. I constantly felt anger even if I didn't know you and you were a stranger. After being to jail a few times, they told me nothing's going to change me.

I have to learn that I don't need to live my past, and that I should try something new. There are lots of criminals, but the ones that make it are few.

And here comes the moral of the story on cue, even if the system didn't help me, doesn't mean it can't help you. And even if in the beginning of life you had a bad start, it doesn't mean from the beginning to the end that you can't live with a good heart. Never compare yourself with anyone else, just be yourself and remember, just because someone else can't do it, doesn't mean that you can't make the choice to do it.

Hope

Hope is the rack which I hang my dreams upon, carefully placing one article of my future on.

Hope is the box which I place my thoughts in, gingerly folding my aspirations into.

Hope is the shelf on which I stick my fears on, cautiously tucking them away from striving.

Hope is where I hang my success on proudly displaying all I have accomplished with the help of hope.

Believe In Yourself

Set your standards high, you deserve the best. Try for what you want and never settle for less. Believe in yourself no matter what you choose.

Keep a winning attitude and you can never lose. Think about your destination but don't worry if you stray, because the most important thing is what you've learned along the way. Take all that you've come to be, all that you can be. Soar above the clouds and let your dreams set you free.

Figure U9.2 Mural, "Love, Peace & Harmony," by Jesse T., Kyle P., Tony D., Carol Cross, Bryce H. (15′ × 8′)

Photograph by Carol Cross.

Discussion

The topic is self-betrayal. Let us look within ourselves and reconstruct some of the events that have brought us here.

How can life be different this time around?

What changes do you need or want to make?

Can people change? What can stop you or hold you back?

What will help YOU succeed?

Writing Ideas

Where do you see yourself in the future? Next year? Five years from now?

Identify supports—people who can help you achieve your goals.

Write a letter to yourself about what you think is important in life, like the things that you enjoy and that keep you positive when you are feeling down. Make a list AND try to make this list as long as you can.

Use the space for *your* self-portrait.

Figure U9.3 Mural, Pacific Mid Coast, Kneeling human releasing a hummingbird (53′ × 39′) by Alex M., Carol Cross, Chris J., Cody J., David C.

Photograph by Carol Cross.

THIS IS YOUR WORKBOOK. GIVE IT A TITLE AND CONTINUE TO ADD YOUR WRITINGS AND ARTWORK.

Index

Page numbers in *italics* indicate figures

"A." 50–51
abuse 2, 3, 4–5, 10, 11–13, 18, 20, 30, 34, 38, 39
accommodation 2
accountability 20, 27–28, 35, 36
adaptation 2–3
aftercare services 25
alcohol 7, 51
alternative learning centers (ALCs) 34–35
American Psychological Association (APA) 5
Americans for the Arts 6
anti-psychotics 5
antisocial personality disorder 16
anxiety 5, 16, 23
Arctic Rose Foundation 35
assimilation 2
attention deficit hyperactivity disorder (ADHD) 5, 16

Bailey, S. 12
Barlinnie Prison 43
The Beat Within 30
behavior modification 18
Bennett, Theresa 52, 53, 55
Bertram, Chris 15
Biehler, R. 2, 63
Black, Indigenous, People of Color (BIPOC) 15–16, 21
body art 55
bullying 5
Bumgarner Gee, Constance M. 5–6
Burnham, Linda 3

"C." 23–24, 51
"C. D." *52*
"C. J." 10, *57*
"C. R." *57*
Carrell, C. 43
Champions of Change 6
cognitive conflict 2–3
Cohen, Albert K. 19
collaborative projects 6, 30, 63–65
community 72; engaged learning 38–40, justice 25, 27–32, programs ix, 29, 33–41, 66–67, regeneration 27–32, 66
Congdon, K. G. 17, 34
Constructivism 1, 59, 63
coping skills 3, 20–21, 23
Correctional Services Canada (CSC) 16, 19, 47
counseling programs 3
Crimson Tears 11
Cross, Carol 15, 36, 38, 40, 50, 55, 57, 61, *64*, 75, 76
cultural awareness 40, 58
culturally responsive programs 30
culturally-Sensitive Support 15–16
culture 16–17
Currie, E. 5, 19

Davis, Angela 12, 18, 29
DeBellis, M. D. 2
Delgado, M. 15, 35
democracy 3, 59
depression 5, 16, 18, 23
Dewey, John 1, 67
drugs 7, 22, 51

Efland, A 11
Eisner, E. W. 33
emotional development 28–29
emotional intelligence 28
empathy 28, 67
empowerment 1, 23, 24, 25, 27, 39, 46–47, 63, 65, 67, 72
empowerment theory 35–36
Evan-Egar, E. 11

Everyone Deserves Growth & Empowerment (EDGE) 47
existential intelligence 28–29
experiential learning 47

Fetal Alcohol Syndrome Disorder (FASD) 14–15, 16
Fine, G. A. 17
foster care ix, 12, 19, 61
Foucault, Michel 2, 18–19
Fuentes, Rafael 75

gang life 22–23, 66
gangster persona 19
Gardner, H. 28–29, 61
Garland, D. 28
Gignac, Sarah 37–38
Giroux, H. A. 3, 5, 33–34, 61
Give Yourself a Chance 50–51
The Globe and Mail 15
Goldfarb, Brian 36
Goleman, Daniel 6, 28, 29
Gude, Olivia 56

Harris, M. 17
Healing Lodge programs 16
Heath, S. B. 2, 36
Herman, C. A. 23
Herman, Judith 4
Hillman, Grady 11
hooks, b. 1, 8
'Horror-scopes' 48, *49*

Indigenous people 13, 15–16, 30, 35, 58, 75
Inside-Out Magazine 11, 22, 30, 42, 43–51, *45*, *49*, 56, 73–76
intelligence 61
Intensive Rehabilitative Custody and Supervision (IRCS) Order 14
intergenerational trauma 13
It's Just the Way I am 51
It's Not Too Late 35

J. D. 3
Jackson, Jesse L. Sr. 27, 28, 29, 66
"Jason" 15
Journal of Adolescent Health 5
journals 2

Kamler, Richard 65
Kelly 11
Kids of Survival (K.O.S) 7
Kleinman, S. 17
Kools, Susan 12
Kornfeld, Phyllis 34
Kornfield, Jack 36, 61
"K.'s" story 11
Kurtz, Z. R. 12

Laing, J. 43
language problems 2
Learning by Designing 58
Leave Out Violence 4, 7, 36–38, 42
Lipsey, M. W. 3
Long-term Inmates Now in the Community (LINC) 47
Lorde, A. 33, 44

McCreary Centre Society 13
McFee, J. K. 1
McLuhan, Marshall 73
Management and Trainings Corporation 29
Mansbridge, J. 3
Massachusetts Youth Screening Instrument-2 (MAYSI-2) 10
Mayer, John 28
medical model 72
mental health 12, 43, 65; social inclusion 31, support 4, 23–24
mentoring 3, 22, 23, 40, 47–48, 63
Messy Book Program 35
Molad, B. 42
Monday Magazine 37–38
Morrison, T. 2
Morven, Frank 14–15
The Mural Project 13, 30, 42, 46, 48, 56–58, *57*, *75*

National Symposium on Art Education 7
Nelson Mandela Rules 16
The New Yorker 4–5
Noam, G. G. 4, 23, 42
non-suicidal self-injury (NSSI) 5

organization 2
"O's" story 7
Out of Bounds 47, 48, 71–74
The Outside Guide 24–25, 42, 58–60, *59–60*, *63*, *64*

Parsons, M. 3
Patrick (Pat) R. 3, 47–48, 71–74
peers 24–25, 59; education 4, 35–36, mentors 22, 63, support 46, 48
Piaget, Jean 2, 61
post-traumatic stress disorder (PTSD) 10, 18, 19–21, 23, 29
prison art programs 42–44
private corporations 29–30
punishment model 14, 23

rap music 24, 51
Reality on the Inside 23–24, 44, 46
recovery 3–4
release planning 13
resilience 3–4, 35
responsibility 20, 27–28, 35, 36
restorative justice 3, 14, 47
Rettig, R. P. 18, 21
Rhein, A. 42
Richmond, J. 28, 35, 36
Ritalin 5
Roach, A. 2, 36
Rollins, Tim 7

safe environments 4, 6–7, 14, 20, 23, 31, 39–40, 42, 66
Salovey, Peter 28
Scarth, Andrea 14
school-based intervention programs 4
segregation 18
self-esteem 7, 20, 34, 48, 65, 66, 73
self-harm 18
self-identity 12, 23, 30, 66
self-injury 5, 11
self-portraits 52–53, *53*
skill building programs 3
Smith, R. 58
Snowman, H. 2, 63
social activism 67
social engagement 34
social inclusion 31
social intelligence 30
social justice 10–26, 33
social learning 39–40
social support 22, 31, 43, 46
sock monkey project *55*
Soep, E. 2, 36
Solomon, Andrew 4–5
The Special Unit, Barlinnie Prison 43
Stokrocki, Mary 17
subculture 17, 18–19, 25
substance use disorder 21–23
suicide 4–5, 15
The Sunday Art + Design Group 42, 52–55

"T." 22
"T. S" 17

talk therapy 31
tattoos 5, *55*
Think of Us 38
Thornes, R. 12
Thrive Collective xi
'time out' 18
Tupac 51, *52*
Tye S. 76

United Nations 16
United Nations International Children's Fund (UNICEF) 35

Vancouver Island 59–60, 63
Victoria Youth Custody Centre (VYCC) 50–51, *59*, *75*
violence 4, 12, 18, 20, 34–36, 43, 66; by women 17, cycle ix, Leave Out Violence 4, 7, 36–38, 42, PTSD 10, 23, 29, Youth Violence Intervention Program 47
Voices Unbroken 35
Vygotsky, Lev 1

Waldram, J. 16
Wasserman, G. A. ix
welfare system 4, 38
wellbeing 11, 65
Westhaven-Elmhurst Community Recreation Association (WECRA) 38–40
Wilcock, A. A. 11
Wilde, Oscar 71, 74
William Head Penitentiary 47, 71–74
William Head on Stage (WHoS) 71
Winner, K. 42
women, violence 17

Youth Criminal Justice Act (YCJA) 13–14, 16, 20, 27
youth development theory 21
youth participatory action research (YPAR) 42
youth reentry 65
Youth Risk Behavior Survey 5
Youth Violence Intervention Program (YVIP) 47

zero tolerance 27
Zimmerman, Marc 35–36

For Product Safety Concerns and Information please contact our
EU representative GPSR@taylorandfrancis.com Taylor & Francis
Verlag GmbH, Kaufingerstraße 24, 80331 München, Germany